A Collection of Plays

By Joseph Rubanoff

Volume One

For my talented daughter,
writer/actress, Annie Wood, who made
these collections possible.

List of Plays

Winner of ALAP monthly reading contest.

UNINTENDED CONSEQUENCES

A play in two acts

MAX, an elderly man

LINDA, a young woman.

The rear deck of a luxurious hillside home in Los
Angeles. It is a beautiful summer morning. At rise
Linda, a young woman, enters from the interior of the
house immediately followed by Max, an elderly man.
Excited, she rushes to the railing and looks out.

>   LINDA
> Oh wow look how beautiful, you can see
> the ocean from here.

>   MAX
> (Amused) And on a clear day, which this
> certainly is, you can see Catalina.

He gestures out over the railing.

>   LINDA
> Yes, I see it. This is fabulous. What I
> wouldn't give to live in a place like
> this. I had no idea.

>   MAX
> Idea about what?

>   LINDA
> You lived in a place like this.

>   MAX
> Oh.

                    LINDA
Just you and your wife live here?

                    MAX
No.

                    LINDA
Oh? I assumed you were...

                    MAX
I'm not married.

                    LINDA
You live here alone?

                    MAX
Yes.

                    LINDA
That's kind of sad.

                    MAX
Sad? Why sad?

                    LINDA
I shouldn't have said that.

                    MAX
Go ahead.

                    LINDA
Well, I mean if you watch the sunrise, or
the sunset, or look up at a sky loaded
with stars, these are things you want to
share with someone special.

                    MAX
I see. You believe life should be shared
with a... significant other?

                    LINDA
Well, yes. And it's sort of a waste, or
empty feeling, I think, when beautiful
moments can't be savored with someone
special.

                    MAX
Okay, I think your idea is not unique.
But that's only one side of the coin,
don't you think?

                    LINDA
What do you mean?

                              MAX
          The other side of the coin is for those
          of us who prefer to be alone.

                              LINDA
          (Dubious) Oh, yeah, I see.

A pause.

                              MAX
          Do you want to get started?

                              LINDA
          Sure.

                              MAX
          You can sit at that round table, if you
          like. And I'll settle into this lounge
          chair.

They sit. She places her tote bag on the table.

She hesitates.

                              MAX (CONT'D)
          Oh, before we start. Maybe you can clear
          up something for me, not that it's really
          important.

                              LINDA
          Okay.

                              MAX
          Yesterday, when we started talking at
          Starbucks, you asked if I would consent
          to be interviewed by you as part of a
          college assignment.

                              LINDA
          Yes.

                              MAX
          At one point, I started thinking about
          this after we parted, I thought you said
          it was for your journalism class, at
          another I understood it was for your
          creative writing class. Maybe my
          confusion comes from the excitement at
          having a pretty young woman initiate a
          conversation with me. Old duffers like
          me are pretty much anonymous.

                    LINDA
I'm sure I wasn't being clear. You see,
I haven't selected my major yet. But I do
know I want to be a writer. So I am
taking journalism and creative writing
classes. My assignment is to interview
an elderly person and write about it for
my creative writing class.

                    MAX
All right. And that interview is about
to begin.

                    LINDA
Yes. (Hesitates) Although, it could be
more than one interview, if you're
willing?

                    MAX
We'll see.

                    LINDA
You see, this is a term project. How we
handle the material, as a series of
questions and answers and our
impressions, or write a novella, or
whatever, is our choice. We were urged to
be as creative and as innovative as we
wished. The length and the form and even
if it develops into more fiction than
nonfiction is entirely up to the writer.

                    MAX
I have a hunch that's usually the case.
And remember, you agreed, I could
interview you, too.

                    LINDA
(Laughs) Okay, but I'm pretty young, not
much has happened in my life.

                    MAX
Then I'll interview you mostly about your
future.

                    LINDA
The future? How can you do that?

                    MAX
By being creative and innovative?

                         LINDA
          I think you're teasing me, aren't you?
          My instructor, Mr. Parker, said our
          purpose was to try to get at and reveal
          the very essence of the subject's life.

                         MAX
          I think you'll make Mr. Parker proud.

He motions for her to proceed with the interview. She
removes a tape recorder from her tote bag and places it
on the table.

                         MAX (CONT'D)
          Is that a tape recorder?

                         LINDA
          Yes, is it all right? I wouldn't have
          turned it on without your permission.

                         MAX
          Let's defer that for the present. I'll
          probably change my mind later. I think
          it could even interfere with your
          "creative process."

                         LINDA
          All right.

She puts the cassette into the tote bag. A pause.

                         LINDA (CONT'D)
          It's a little awkward starting.

                         MAX
          Take your time.

                         LINDA
          I never thought, when the time came to
          start, I'd be, well, a little shy about
          it.

                         MAX
          It's okay. I think you'll soon overcome
          your shyness.

                         LINDA
          Will it be okay with you if my questions
          don't follow any particular pattern, if I
          just kind of skip around?

                         MAX
          Fine.

                    LINDA
          That's okay then?

                    MAX
          Seems like a good technique. Like a
          lawyer conducting a cross-examination,
          that can keep the witness off balance,
          one way to get at the truth.

                    LINDA
          Well, I don't want you to be off balance.
          And I think you understand that if any
          question is too personal, or you just
          don't care to answer, you can just say
          no.

                    MAX
          Sure, that's understood.

She is about to speak.

                    MAX (CONT'D)
          By the way, there's a small refrigerator
          behind the bar there. (He indicates) It
          has soft drinks, bottled water, etcetera.
          And the refrigerator in the kitchen has
          lots of goodies in it. So just get up
          and help yourself whenever you wish.
          And, if you want to visit the rest room,
          turn left in the hall, first door.

                    LINDA
          Thank you.

                    MAX
          Well, I guess we've covered the
          preliminaries pretty well. Oh, something
          else. Why did you choose me as the
          subject for your interview? Was it
          simply because I was there?

                    LINDA
          You were sitting at your table all alone,
          not doing anything in particular, and, I
          thought, looking a little lonely and
          forlorn.

                    MAX
          Forlorn?

                         LINDA
          Maybe that's the wrong word. And you
          fell into the age range I was looking for
          and I did have my assignment on my mind,
          so I thought I'd ask.

                         MAX
          Thank you. Proceed.

From time to time, Linda jots down something.

                         LINDA
          You said you were not married. Have you
          ever been married?

                         MAX
          Yes.

                         LINDA
          When?

                         MAX
          You want the date of my first marriage?

                         LINDA
          Oh, you've been married more than once?

                         MAX
          Yes.

                         LINDA
          Uh, how many times?

                         MAX
          Four.

                         LINDA
          You've been married four times?

                         MAX
          Yes, four times.

A pause.

                         MAX (CONT'D)
          Okay, I realize I'm giving you a hard
          time by limiting my answers. I could
          have answered your first question by
          simply saying I was married four times
          without making you dig for it. I promise
          to be more expansive with my answers.

                         LINDA
          I'm probably not a very good questioner.

                    MAX
          Linda, somehow I have every confidence in
          your questioning ability.

A pause.

                    LINDA
          Beginning with your first marriage, how
          did each of your marriages end?

                    MAX
          Divorce, divorce, divorce, divorce.

                    LINDA
          How many years have passed since your
          last marriage ended?

                    MAX
          About twenty.

                    LINDA
          Were you living here at that time?

                    MAX
          No, but I bought this house soon after.

                    LINDA
          From the time you bought this house, has
          anyone lived here with you other than say
          guests for brief visits?

                    MAX
               (thinks for a moment. Then,
                crisply)
          No.

                    LINDA
          Do you have children?

                    MAX
          No.

                    LINDA
          In or out of wedlock?

                    MAX
          Hey, Linda, you're getting good at this.
          Very good.

A pause.

                    MAX (CONT'D)
The answer is no, to the best of my
knowledge. Well, I guess the ball's in
my court now.

                    LINDA
What do you mean?

                    MAX
An explanation should be forthcoming, and
I won't even wait for your follow up
questions the tenor of which would be,
*Hey Max, baby, what was going on? Low
sperm count? Impotence? Some other
reason?*

                    LINDA
No, I wouldn't.

                    MAX
It's all right, Linda, it's a fair
question, it had to be asked, and I have
no reluctance answering. A condition of
my marriages was, *no children.*

                    LINDA
Can I ask why?

                    MAX
Sure. Do you know who W.C. Fields was?

                    LINDA
Yes, a comedian. And a movie star.

                    MAX
Did you like him?

                    LINDA
So-so. But I'm not that familiar with
him. He was before my time.

                    MAX
Of course. Well, some people like me,
believe he was a comic genius. Do you
know how he felt about children?

                    LINDA
He pretended that he hated them.

                    MAX
You think he was pretending?

                    LINDA
          It was part of his comic persona, wasn't
          it?

                    MAX
          Suppose he wasn't pretending, and suppose
          I felt the same way?

                    LINDA
          Am I allowed to tell you when I don't
          think you're being candid?

                    MAX
          Why not?

                    LINDA
          I don't think you were candid in what you
          said about children. In fact, I think
          you were being pretentious.

                    MAX
          Whew, you really zinged me on that one,
          Linda. (A beat) Then let's hold the
          matter of children in abeyance for now
          and move on.

                    LINDA
          What was your occupation?

                    MAX
          I have had various occupations, such as I
          was a lawyer for a while, and a judge for
          a while, but mostly I've been an
          entrepreneur.

A pause. Both realize this answer has opened up a large
area to explore. They exchange a knowing look.

                    LINDA
          How long were you a lawyer?

                    MAX
          About fifteen years.

                    LINDA
          How long were you a judge?

                    MAX
          About seven years. And following that
          law stuff, most of my life I was an
          entrepreneur.

                    LINDA
          Why did you stop being a judge?

                    MAX
Ouch. (A beat) That opens up a can of
worms.

                    LINDA
How so?

                    MAX
I resigned. A forced resignation so to
speak. Under a cloud. I had my critics,
enemies, who felt I had crossed that
sometimes amorphous line of ethical and
strictly legal conduct.

                    LINDA
Did you cross the line?

                    MAX
Let me answer this way, at the risk of
sounding pretentious again...

                    LINDA
I want to apologize for what I said. It
was uncalled for. I'm really sorry.

                    MAX
You landed a solid punch to the solar
plexus. Accurate, painful. Necessary?
I admire your gumption. I think. And
now, for my next pretentious moment:
Where do you draw the line? There it is
in a nutshell. That's the question in all
human relationships, in the law, in all
conduct between individuals,
institutions, nations.

                    LINDA
And so getting back to my question, did
you cross the line?

                    MAX
(Bemused) Careful, Linda, you're getting
too good at posing hard questions.

                    LINDA
It's clear you don't want to answer the
question.
        (beat)
I promise not to make judgmental comments
anymore.

                    MAX
Can you resist?

                    LINDA
I'll try.

                    MAX
Back to your question, I probably screwed
up.

                    LINDA
Probably?

                    MAX
I stayed out of jail. The situation was
not so clear cut. And of course judges
would rather look the other way when
there's a potential problem of "wrong
doing" in the ranks.

                    LINDA
I still haven't succeeded in getting a
straight answer. I don't think you
intend to answer my question now.

                    MAX
Right.

A pause.

                    LINDA
Mr. Simon, if you don't want to continue
with what we're doing, you don't have to.

                    MAX
I know that, Linda. I definitely do want
to continue. And, although I don't
generally like it when young people
address me by my first name, I'm going to
ask you to address me as Max.

                    LINDA
All right, Max.

                    MAX
And now I have to ask you to refresh my
memory. I forgot your last name.

                    LINDA
It's Lane.

                    MAX
Lane. Linda Lane. Sounds like the type
of name the movie studios used to give to
their starlets.

                    LINDA
It is a made up name. I made it up.

                    MAX
Can we shift gears now, and maybe I can
ask you a few questions?

                    LINDA
Okay.

                    MAX
Have you always lived in Los Angeles?

                    LINDA
Yes.

                    MAX
I'm assuming you're not married.

                    LINDA
Yes.

                    MAX
What does your father do for a living?

                    LINDA
I don't know, I never met him.

                    MAX
Tell me about your mother.

                    LINDA
She died before I was three. I was
raised by my grandmother.

                    MAX
Tell me about your grandmother.

                    LINDA
We never got along. I left three years
ago. We're not in touch.

                    MAX
That doesn't sound like a happy childhood
to me.

                    LINDA
It wasn't.

                    MAX
How do you get by now?

                    LINDA
I manage.

                    MAX
          Not a terribly responsive answer. You're
          not a good role model for me if you don't
          answer forthrightly.

                    LINDA
          I'll try to do better.

                    MAX
          Are you really a college student?

                    LINDA
          Of course.

Abruptly, she rises and starts to put her notebook in her
tote bag.

                    LINDA (CONT'D)
          If you don't believe me, what's the
          point?

                    MAX
          My, you are touchy. Sit down. Oh, sit
          down, Linda!

She sits.

                    MAX (CONT'D)
          Let's refine the rules we operate under.
          Let us agree we are entitled to make very
          frank exchanges, when the spirit moves
          us. Not that we should abandon the rule
          of civilized conduct, no, not at all,
          but...

                    LINDA
          ... all right.

                    MAX
          Why don't we take a break now. And
          perhaps a snack?

                    LINDA
          You must have heard my stomach growling,
          I'm starving.

He starts to get out the lounge chair. It's a bit of an
effort.

                    LINDA (CONT'D)
          Can I give you a hand?

Max gets up.

                          MAX
          I made it. Tell you what, I need ten,
          fifteen minutes to myself. If this isn't
          too sexist, why don't you go into the
          kitchen, grab a tray and dishes and bring
          some edibles out here? Lot's of things
          in the refrigerator that don't need any
          preparation.

Max is at the door, he says, expansively...

                          MAX (CONT'D)
          Mi casa es su casa.

He exits to the house. Her eyes follow him. Then she
casts her eyes all about the deck and out into the
distance. She turns and exits to the house.

BLACKOUT.

Lights up: Twenty minutes later. Linda and Max are
seated at the round table, eating.

                          LINDA
          Everything's so delicious.

                          MAX
          I'm glad.

                          LINDA
          So many delicious salads and stuff. Did
          you prepare any of this?

                          MAX
          No. Food preparation is not one of my
          strengths.

                          LINDA
          What do you consider your strengths to
          be?

                          MAX
          (Playful) Oh, what a dandy question, but
          potentially very embarrassing.

                          LINDA
          Why embarrassing?

                          MAX
          Suppose I have no strengths?

                          LINDA
          Everyone does.

                    MAX
Then suppose they are of such a minor
nature, it's pathetic to even mention
them?

                    LINDA
Then maybe I'll revise my question and
ask, what are your talents?

                    MAX
Heavens, that could be even more
embarrassing. (Thinks) A long time ago,
I played the violin. But the less said
about that, the better.

                    LINDA
(Laughs) You have a good sense of humor.

                    MAX
I do? You have, I think, an intuitive
grasp of things, but I think you just
missed the plaintive quality of my
answers.

                    LINDA
I think a man who has been a lawyer, and
a judge, and an "entrepreneur" can't be
entirely lacking in strengths and talent.

He smiles enigmatically. A pause.

                    LINDA (CONT'D)
I may have to leave pretty soon. Do you
think it would be okay if I came again
tomorrow?

                    MAX
All right. But I was wondering, don't
you have classes to attend?

                    LINDA
I'm pretty selective about my classroom
attendance.

                    MAX
Do you think the school administration is
as selective?

                    LINDA
(Shrugs) I guess we're getting into the
area of where do you draw the line?

                    MAX
          I can't fault you for not paying
          attention to what I say.

                    LINDA
          I'd rather not leave yet, but I have an
          afternoon job.

                    MAX
          Oh, where do you work?

                    LINDA
          McDonalds.

                    MAX
          McDonalds?

                    LINDA
          McDonalds.

                    MAX
          Linda, how old are you?

                    LINDA
          Twenty.

                    MAX
          I would have guessed a little older.

                    LINDA
          Well, as it happens, I'll be twenty-one
          tomorrow.

                    MAX
          Then I missed being right by one day.

                    LINDA
          Close, but no cigar.

                    MAX
          Have you made plans to celebrate your
          birthday?

                    MAX (CONT'D)
          Just to come here.

A Pause.

                    MAX (CONT'D)
          Why do you want to be a writer?

                    LINDA
          I don't know. Mostly, it's just a strong
          feeling I have. Did you have a strong
          feeling to take up the law?

                    MAX
          I don't remember.

                    LINDA
          You must. If it wasn't a strong feeling,
          then it must have been a calculation that
          it was the thing to do to get ahead in
          life, or to make money.

                    MAX
          Linda, you don't cease to amaze by your
          precociousness.

                    LINDA
          That's a word to apply to children. Me,
          I was emancipated almost three years ago
          to the day.

                    MAX
          Emancipated. Now that's a lawyer-like
          word.

                    LINDA
          It was the appropriate word to say what I
          wanted to say.

A pause.

                    MAX
          Don't you want to do something special
          tomorrow, be with your friends?

                    LINDA
          I don't have friends. I'm kind of a
          loner, Max.

                    MAX
          Hmmm. So am I. Fate, it seems, has
          introduced us.

                    LINDA
          I thought it was more my doing.

                    MAX
          Don't you think fate works in mysterious
          way?

The phone rings. Max answers.

                    MAX (CONT'D)
              (on phone)
Hello. No! I said no! Don't ever call
me again!

Max hangs up the phone.

                    MAX (CONT'D)
Goddamn telemarketers!

                    LINDA
So you do have a temper.

                    MAX
Why did you doubt it?

                    LINDA
You sure kept it in check when I was
disrespectful and insulting.

                    MAX
Was that a test? And if so, did I pass
or fail?

                    LINDA
I didn't come here to test you, just to
discover who you were. Are. It must be
so fascinating to be your age, to be able
to look back at most of your life.

                    MAX
You think I'm at a fascinating stage of
my life?

                    LINDA
Oh, yes. Whenever I see elderly people I
wonder what do they think about, are they
constantly replaying and critiquing their
past? Does remorse trump happy memories?
And what do they think about their waning
future? Are they scared? Or welcoming
perhaps? Or are they just preoccupied
with the minutiae of day to day living?

                    MAX
(Impressed) You have excellent verbal
skills. If that holds for your writing
skills, you should do well.

                    LINDA
Thank you.

                    MAX
You may also have a future as a coroner.
You could have such happy colloquies with
your corpses as you dissect them.

                    LINDA
Max, do you think I'm too cold and
calculating?

                    MAX
That certainly was not my first
impression. I thought you were quite an
innocent. But, Linda, more and more I am
thinking you are an amazing piece of
work.

A pause.

                    LINDA
I think I should be going.

                    MAX
To McDonalds?

                    LINDA
To McDonalds.

                    MAX
In all my life, I have never been inside
a McDonalds.

                    LINDA
Then I want you to come one day as my
guest in exchange for your hospitality.
(She gestures toward the round table) But
we're not famous for such gourmet
tidbits.

                    MAX
So I've heard.

They are on their feet now.

                    LINDA
Tomorrow at about the same time?

                    MAX
All right. Drive carefully. Watch the
narrow curves going down.

                    LINDA
Oh, I didn't drive.

                         MAX
          Then how did you get up here?

                         LINDA
          I hitchhiked on Sunset Boulevard and then
          I hiked up the rest of the way.

                         MAX
          That's quite a trek. It's really hard to
          believe.

                         LINDA
          Believe, Max, believe.

He follows her into the house.

                         LINDA (CONT'D)
          Goodbye, Max, see you tomorrow.

                         MAX
          Okay, Linda, I'll expect you about the
          same time.

O.S. Sound of door closing. A beat.

                         MAX (CONT'D)
          JESUS CHRIST!!!!!!!!

BLACKOUT.

Lights up: The next morning. A hazy morning. Linda and
Max enter exactly as the previous morning. Linda is
wearing the same clothing. Linda goes directly to the
railing and looks out in the direction of Catalina.

                         LINDA
          It's hazy, I can't see Catalina this
          morning.

                         MAX
          It's still there, I'm sure, or we would
          have been notified. (He studies her) I'm
          looking to see if you're out of breath,
          which would be only natural if you walked
          up from Sunset Blvd. I don't see any
          signs of huffing and puffing.

                         LINDA
          I got lucky today. I got a ride on
          Sunset and persuaded the driver to drop
          me off right in front of the house.

As they speak, she sits again at the round table, and he
lowers himself into his lounge chair.

                    MAX
There are a number of things I've been
thinking about since you left yesterday,
and the subject of hitchhiking is right
at the top of my list. Don't you think,
especially in this day and age, that
hitchhiking is extremely dangerous?

                    LINDA
I'm not afraid.

                    MAX
You should be.

                    LINDA
I don't have the luxury of being afraid.

                    MAX
I see, they don't pay a luxurious wage at
McDonalds.

They laugh.

                    LINDA
And what else were you thinking about?

                    MAX
I'm not exactly ready to leave the
subject of your transportation... but all
right, we'll come back to it. (Beat)
What else was I thinking? I've been
trying to reconstruct in my mind all the
circumstances of our meeting at
Starbucks. The question I've been
pondering is who got there first? You or
me?

                    LINDA
Why is that important?

                    MAX
It's important to me to fill in even
little gaps in my memory, to clear up
even minor confusion. When I do, I feel
I'm holding the fort against advancing
dementia.

                    LINDA
Well, if you're trying to remember who
got to Starbucks first, I'm not so clear
on that either. So am I fighting
advancing dementia, too?

                    MAX
If you are, I think you'll win.

                    LINDA
I sure don't see any evidence of anything
wrong with your mind.

                    MAX
That may be because I'm a tricky fellow,
a past master at concealing the evidence.

                    LINDA
Yeah, well I'm not so gullible. (Beat)
Okay, what's your first guess as to who
was first?

                    MAX
I believe you were already sitting out
there when I drove up. I parked right
out front so you couldn't have missed
seeing me arrive.

                    LINDA
I don't know. I spent a lot of time
there that day, but I was doing my
homework and I had my head buried in my
work. On the other hand, I'm usually
aware of what's going on around me, and I
don't think I would have missed you if
you parked out front just a few feet
away.

                    MAX
I, too, am usually aware of my
surroundings, and I don't think I would
have failed to notice you sitting there,
even with your head buried in a book.
Still, I am inclined to think you were
there, but because I couldn't see your
pretty face, it didn't register. So what
have we here? A mystery of sorts?

                    LINDA
Not necessarily. I was out there a long
time. After a while, I got hungry and
went inside to buy a muffin. It took a
while because I had to wait in line.
That may be when you arrived.

                    LINDA (CONT'D)
(A beat) Oh, yes, that's it I'm sure.
You didn't go inside because you didn't
have anything on your table.
                    (MORE)

                    LINDA (CONT'D)
After we started talking and I joined you
at your table, I remember thinking it was
kind of strange that you were sitting out
there at a table without purchasing
anything.

                    MAX
I really don't like their coffee.

                    LINDA
So, Max, do you mind telling me what this
little exercise has been about?

                    MAX
It's not terribly important.

                    LINDA
Come on, tell me.

A pause. He is thinking.

                    MAX
Do you know what kind of car I drive?

                    LINDA
No. Should I?

                    MAX
It's a Bentley.

                    LINDA
I'm not into cars. Should I be
impressed?

                    MAX
Even here in the Beverly Hills area, a
land of expensive cars, people stop to
look and to comment when they see my car.

                    LINDA
Your point being?

                    MAX
My point being, and this is sheer
speculation you understand, you could
have seen this handsome, elegant, old
gentleman...

Max points to himself.

                    MAX (CONT'D)
... Arrive in his car, and understandably
have thought, *that is one rich dude.*

A long pause. Linda is simmering, Max is watching her
closely.

                    LINDA
          So that's it. Yesterday, you accused me
          of not being a college student. Today,
          it's far worse, I'm conducting some kind
          of scam, and you are my mark. Is that
          the way it goes, Max?

He shrugs but remains silent.

                    LINDA (CONT'D)
          Oh, come on, Max, admit it. Your
          scenario is - Linda hangs out in an
          upscale neighborhood, Linda identifies
          her victim, gains his confidence, gets
          invited into his house on some pretext
          and then...

Max remains silent. Linda rises.

                    LINDA (CONT'D)
          The interview is over. Mission
          accomplished. I have discovered your
          true essence. You are a world class
          shmuck! Fuck you, Max!

She wheels around and storms out of the room. O.S. The
front door is heard slamming shut.

                    MAX
          (Unperturbed) But, Dearie, you left
          your tote bag behind, so you'll be back,
          won't you?

He stares at the bag.

                    MAX (CONT'D)
          Well, I must overcome my scruples and
          seize the opportunity.

He rummages in the tote bag and removes her wallet. He
looks inside.

                    MAX (CONT'D)
          Let's see, two one dollar bills. No
          credit cards. Looks like genuine poverty
          to me. McDonalds, you will have to start
          paying a living wage.

                    MAX (CONT'D)
          What have we here?

He removes a driver's license, studies it.

>   MAX (CONT'D)
>   Sadie Kupotel? What the hell kind of
>   name is that? No wonder she changed it
>   to Linda Lane. But it's hers, it's her
>   picture.
>   And let's see... Yes, today is her
>   birthday but... let me do the date of
>   birth arithmetic. Aha, she's twenty
>   five. Naughty, naughty.

He re-inserts the driver's license and replaces the
wallet. He removes the tape recorder, studies it.

>   MAX (CONT'D)
>   Well, maybe I'll get lucky.

He switches it on. We hear Linda's voice on the machine.

>   LINDA (V.O.)
>   My first interview with Max Simon. He
>   lives alone in a fabulous house with a
>   fabulous view. He has a certain amount
>   of charm at times but somehow I don't
>   trust him. There is something about him
>   that doesn't quite track. Yes, I'm sure
>   he's not sincere and I doubt any of his
>   answers are truthful. I think this is
>   all a game to him and he's just playing
>   along for his own amusement. Sometimes,
>   I really feel ill at ease with him...

O.S the front door chimes are heard followed by knocking.

>   LINDA (V.O.)
>   ... Even when he is being pleasant.

He switches off the cassette.

>   MAX
>   Now I wonder who that could be.

He replaces the cassette in Linda's tote bag and arranges
the bag on the table exactly as she left it.

He exits to the living room, inside.

>   LINDA (O.S.)
>   I forgot my bag.

>   MAX (O.S.)
>   Go ahead and get it. And wait there a
>   minute.

Linda enters the balcony, snatches her bag from the
table, hesitates for a moment and then turns to leave.
Max enters, both arms extended bearing a very large sheet
cake.

                    MAX
          Happy birthday, Linda.

                    LINDA
          What's that?

                    MAX
          A birthday cake.

                    LINDA
          What am I supposed to do with that?

                    MAX
          Eat it, of course. This is no ordinary
          cake, cherries and chocolate mouse and
          whipped cream, quite decadent.

                    LINDA
          You could feed an army with that.

                    MAX
          Share it with your... co-workers.

She hesitates, almost relents, then stiffens.

                    LINDA
          You know what, Max. Shove it up your ass!

She wheels around and exits. O.S. The front door is
heard slamming shut. Max looks at the cake, ruefully.

                    MAX
          But that's not the usual starting place
          in the alimentary canal.

BLACKOUT

Lights up: The following morning. Linda enters, followed
by Max. She is still wearing the same clothing. Linda
stops near the round table.

                    LINDA
          Thank you for allowing me to come. I
          wanted...

>   MAX
>   You haven't looked out at Catalina.
>   That's part of our tradition.

>   LINDA
>   Tradition? I've only been here twice
>   before.

>   MAX
>   At my age, traditions must be developed
>   quickly.

She goes to the rail, looks out.

>   LINDA
>   Yes, I see it today.

>   MAX
>   You see, Catalina is still there. That
>   must serve as a metaphor for something.

Linda approaches him.

>   LINDA
>   Thanks for agreeing to see me. I'll only
>   be a minute. I just had to apologize to
>   you in person. I thought of doing it on
>   the phone, or writing you a letter of
>   apology, but that would have been a cop
>   out. There was no justification for what
>   I did and I sincerely apologize. You
>   didn't deserve that from me. I'm so
>   sorry. I'll go now.

>   MAX
>   Okay, Linda, now sit down.

Linda hesitates.

>   MAX (CONT'D)
>   Please sit down.

She sits at the round table. He sits down at the table.

>   MAX (CONT'D)
>   I accept your apology. Now I will
>   apologize to you.

>   LINDA
>   What for?

>   MAX
>   I manipulated you, I provoked you. I'm
>   very good at that.
>   (MORE)

                    MAX (CONT'D)
While you may have some issues with anger
management, I have issues with anger
incitement. So lets wipe the slate
clean.

He extends his hand for a handshake. She hesitates, then
shakes hands with him.

                    MAX (CONT'D)
We need to make some changes in our
relationship... more honesty. Now I don't
expect either one of us will go all the
way in that direction, that might be
rash. But we must demonstrate progress.

                    LINDA
I have been honest.

                    MAX
(Wags his finger) Uh, uh, uh. Now,
you're not really a college student, are
you? And no histrionics this time.

                    LINDA
Well, I tried to enroll. But the classes
I wanted were already full. I did audit
some classes for a day or two. That's
how I knew about the term paper
assignment.

                    MAX
And you don't really work for McDonalds,
do you?

                    LINDA
I did a while back. It didn't pan out.
How did you know?

                    MAX
I know.

                    LINDA
How?

                    MAX
It's something you do when you're lying.

                    LINDA
What?

                    MAX
I'm not going to tell you. Does that
make you uncomfortable?

                    LINDA
          Yes.

He shrugs, an expression of "too bad." A long pause.

                    MAX
          Something must be done about your
          situation.

                    LINDA
          What situation?

                    MAX
          Oh, come on, Linda.

                    LINDA
          I don't know what you're talking about.

                    MAX
          Then I'll enlighten you. (A beat and
          then quickly) Where do you live now?

                    LINDA
          What's that have to do with anything?

                    MAX
          Tell me where you live.

                    LINDA
          (Reluctantly) In a shelter. A shelter
          for homeless women.

                    MAX
          You have some personal possessions there
          now?

                    LINDA
          Yes.

                    MAX
          Are they worth retrieving?

                    LINDA
          Some things I'd like to have.

                    MAX
          We can send for them.

                    LINDA
          I'd like to know what this is all about.

                    MAX
          Yes, you have a point. I am putting the
          cart before the horse.
                    (MORE)

                    MAX (CONT'D)
All right, Linda, it's clear that you are
destitute. You need a job, a job right
now, that pays a decent wage. I am going
to offer you a job.

                    LINDA
Doing what?

                    MAX
I need a housekeeper, cook, personal
assistant, let's call it my girl Friday,
all rolled into one.

                    LINDA
And you're offering that job to me?

                    MAX
Yes.

                    LINDA
That's the most ridiculous thing I've
heard in my life.

                    MAX
Ridiculous? Just ridiculous? It's
absurd, ludicrous, irrational. That's
why I think it may work out.

                    LINDA
I can't do any of those things.

                    MAX
Yes you can.

                    LINDA
I can tell how clean and orderly
everything here is. I don't think I can
do that.

                    MAX
You have the road map to follow, just
follow it, meticulously.

                    LINDA
You're not serious. This is all a joke
to you.

                    MAX
I am serious.

                    LINDA
What happened to the person who has been
doing all this for you?

                    MAX
        Senora Ramirez. Alas, she had to return
        to Salvador. Her parents are very ill,
        her family there is in chaos. She
        doesn't have a clue when she can return.

                    LINDA
        Did she live here?

                    MAX
        Not at first. But it evolved into that.

                    LINDA
        Evolved?

                    MAX
        Yes.

                    LINDA
        (Suspicious) Do I have to live here?

                    MAX
        The job includes free room and board.
        There is a neat little maid's room, and
        three other unoccupied, nicely furnished
        bedrooms, each with private bath. Take
        your pick.

She is thinking.

                    LINDA
        I'm tempted.

Max rises.

                    MAX
        Think it over. I'll be back in a minute.
        Or two.

He exits. She looks about, covetously. Then she sits,
trance-like, and waits. After a few moments, Max
returns. He has a tray with two plates on which are
slices of cake. He serves her and himself, sits.

                    MAX (CONT'D)
        This is your birthday cake.

                    LINDA
        Thanks.

They eat slowly, methodically.

                    LINDA (CONT'D)
        This is wonderful.

He nods. They are silent as they continue to eat.

>   LINDA (CONT'D)
>   How much are you going to pay me?

>   MAX
>   Oh? Funny, I hadn't really given it any
>   thought.

She is waiting for his answer.

>   MAX (CONT'D)
>   Okay, how much did they pay you at
>   McDonalds?

>   LINDA
>   Two hundred dollars a week.

>   MAX
>   Fine, I'll double that.

>   LINDA
>   (Excited)Four hundred dollars a week?

>   MAX
>   Yes. (A beat) Suppose I pay your first
>   week in advance, in case you decide you
>   want to add a few items to your wardrobe?

>   LINDA
>   Okay.

>   MAX
>   I'll drop you off. The mall is across
>   the street from Starbucks. I can wait
>   there while you shop.

>   LINDA
>   But you don't like their coffee.

>   MAX
>   What the hell, I enjoy sitting there.

>   LINDA
>   Why are you doing this for me?

>   MAX
>   Why not? I have my reasons, of course,
>   but so far I haven't discovered what they
>   are.

BLACKOUT

Lights up: Later that afternoon. Max is alone on the
rear deck. He is agitated, pacing.

> MAX (CONT'D)
> GODDAMN IT! GODDAMN IT TO HELL! THAT
> BITCH!

Furious, he continues to pace. After a while, the front
door chimes are heard off stage. He stops in his tracks.

The chimes continue. He goes to the sliding glass door
and leans into the living room.

> MAX (CONT'D)
> (Bellows) The Goddamn front door is
> unlocked!

He steps back out onto the deck. Linda enters. She is
wearing new jeans, a blouse hanging out over her jeans
and sandals. Her face is flushed.

> LINDA
> Max, I'm so sorry. I completely lost
> track of time. I'll bet you're furious.

> MAX
> What the hell is wrong with you? You
> can't do this to me!

> LINDA
> I'm so sorry. I needed so many things. I
> just wasn't thinking. (Half beat) Can I
> show you the things I bought? I left them
> inside.

He does not respond.

> LINDA (CONT'D)
> I am so very sorry. When I got back to
> Starbucks and you weren't there, I
> panicked. I called a cab to drive me up.
> I had just about spent all the money. I
> was short twenty-eight cents on the fare
> and no tip of course. He was not a happy
> camper.

A pause.

> LINDA (CONT'D)
> Max, I was so excited to be able to buy
> things... I needed everything. Being so
> late, it was completely unintentional.
> Why are you still so angry?

                    MAX
     I thought you had run off. I saw that as
     failure, my failure for having misjudged
     you. And your failure for doing such a
     stupid thing. I don't like failure.

                    LINDA
     Failure. I have done a lot of that. But
     I didn't run off, Max, so there was no
     real failure this time.

                    MAX
     This is unacceptable.

A long pause. She looks at him with growing awareness.

                    LINDA
     Do you want me to leave?

He does not reply.

                    LINDA (CONT'D)
     I see, you're unforgiving, aren't you?
     I'll tell you what I'd like to do. I'd
     like to stay here a week. And I'll work
     my ass of and pay back my debt. And then
     I'll leave. Is that acceptable?

He nods yes almost imperceptibly. She turns and exits.

The lights fade.

A few hours later. A lovely, balmy night. Max is
immobile on his lounge chair. Music is playing softly.
Miles Davis or Duke Ellington. After a few moments, the
clang of a gate is heard at stage right. It is at the top
of a small outdoor staircase (unseen) that connects to
the lower level pool area. Linda enters. She is wearing a
short terry beach robe. Her hair is wet, glistening. She
stares down at Max for a while. He may be asleep. Then he
moves slightly.

                    LINDA (CONT'D)
     Can we talk?

After a pause. Max makes a slight assenting movement of
his wrist.

                    MAX
     Talk.

She sits nearby.

LINDA
I won't beat around the bush. I'd like to
remain here for a while longer than just
a week. I'll do anything to stay here.

MAX
Should I take that as an ambiguous or
unambiguous anything?

LINDA
Unambiguous.

MAX
So it appears you've been seduced by a
little comfort.

LINDA
Comfort? It's more than comfort, it's
luxury. I've never experienced luxury
before. I like it. A lot.

MAX
Yes, that's usually the case.

LINDA
You haven't answered.

MAX
I'll take the matter under submission.
Don't get your hopes up.

LINDA
When will I know?

MAX
In due course.

A pause.

MAX (CONT'D)
Aren't you out of character trying to pin
things down in your otherwise chaotic
universe?

LINDA
Yes.

MAX
This could be risky for me. I don't know
you, you could murder me in my sleep.

LINDA
(Grimly) I hereby pledge I will not
murder you in your sleep or at any time.
(MORE)

                         LINDA (CONT'D)
          (A beat) This could be risky for me, too.
          You could be a very abusive man. Are you
          willing to pledge you will not abuse me?

                         MAX
          No. I'd rather keep you in suspense.

                         LINDA
          Maybe you're really a pussy cat.

                         MAX
          Don't bet on it.

She rises.

                         LINDA
          Tomorrow, do you want me to prepare the
          meals?

He appraises her.

                         MAX
          We can order our meals and have them
          delivered.

                         LINDA
          Can I get you something now?

                         MAX
          There's an open bottle of white wine in
          the kitchen refrigerator. Bring it with
          a wine glass.

                         LINDA
          Okay.

Linda begins to leave. Stops.

                         LINDA (CONT'D)
          Would it be all right if I join you?

                         MAX
          No.

                         LINDA
          (Hurt) I'm of age, you know.

                         MAX
          You're not supposed to drink, are you?

                         LINDA
          I never had a serious alcohol problem, it
          was drugs. And I've been clean for two
          years.

                    MAX
          Isn't that what they all say?

                    LINDA
          Sometimes it is the truth, like now. How
          do you know these things?

                    MAX
          I wasn't referring to alcohol or drug
          abuse. You're pregnant, aren't you?

Stunned, she looks down at her stomach, touches it.

                    LINDA
          It shows?

                    MAX
          Either that, or you swallowed a small
          football.

                    LINDA
          I was sure no one would notice yet.

                    MAX
          I saw you down at the pool in your swim
          suit before it got dark. (A beat)
          Noticeable or not, that doesn't alter the
          fact.

                    LINDA
          No, it doesn't.

                    MAX
          If you're gonna get rid of it, it's
          better sooner than later.

                    LINDA
          That's not an option.

                    MAX
          That's your business.

                    LINDA
          Yes.

                    MAX
          Who is the father?

                    LINDA
          I don't know.

                    MAX
          Are you sure about that?

                    LINDA
          I'm sure that I'm sure about that.

                    MAX
          Start making plans. You can only stay
          here a limited time. This is not
          something I want to get involved in.

                    LINDA
          I understand.

                    MAX
          Maybe you can ask for help at that
          shelter where you were staying.

                    LINDA
          I know who to ask, and I know who not to
          ask.

She exits.

BLACKOUT

Lights up: Early the following morning. Linda is alone,
seated at the round table writing rapidly in her
notebook. Max enters. She looks up.

                    LINDA (CONT'D)
          Oh, good morning.

                    MAX
          (Surly) Taking a break?

                    LINDA
          Well, no.

                    MAX
          Run out of things to do?

                    LINDA
          Everything's so spotlessly clean, I
          didn't..

                    MAX
          Don't let that deter you.

                    LINDA
          All right.

She rises.

                    MAX
I want everything kept super clean. My
first impression of you was that you're
probably a slob. If that's true, one of
us is gonna change, and it won't be me.

                    LINDA
(Restraining herself) I'll do my best.
(A beat) Can I get your breakfast now?

                    MAX
My breakfast is cold cereal and fruit. I
handle that myself.

                    LINDA
All right, I'll get started on...

                    MAX
Sit down.

She sits. Max is still grumpy but easing off a bit.

                    MAX (CONT'D)
What were you writing? Still working on
your project about me?

                    LINDA
Yes.

                    MAX
But it's no longer a "school project", is
it?

                    LINDA
I'm doing it for myself.

                    MAX
Do you have more questions for me?

                    LINDA
Lots. But right now, I have more material
than I can handle.

                    MAX
And what's the most important thing
you've learned thus far?

                    LINDA
I've learned that I'm the main character
in this story.

                    MAX
Oh, that's not so good for my ego.

                    LINDA
It's clear I'm not one hundred percent in
control of how this turns out.

                    MAX
Then what's the point of being the
writer?

A pause.

                    LINDA
I wanted to ask you about my duties? You
said you wanted me to be your girl
Friday. What does that mean?

                    MAX
It means you have a variety of duties.
For example, I need to go to the hospital
three times this week for treatment. I'll
need you to drive me, wait for me, and
take me home. And if I'm disabled
briefly, you're my caretaker. Think
you're up to that?

                    LINDA
I'll try. Do you have cancer?

                    MAX
Something in that family.

                    LINDA
Why didn't you tell me instead of letting
it come out this way?

                    MAX
(Laughs) I'm a very crafty fellow,
sometimes I don't even tell myself why I
do things. It's that way with you, too,
isn't it?

                    LINDA
Did Senora Ramirez do all these things
for you?

                    MAX
Yes.

                    LINDA
When did she leave?

                    MAX
Last week.

                    LINDA
          Do you miss her?

                    MAX
          Do I miss her? I had four wives leave me
          and I couldn't care less. (He is very
          emotional) As for her, yes, I miss her
          more than I can say.

                    LINDA
          I know she was your mistress.

He looks at her quizzically.

                    LINDA (CONT'D)
          There was no sign the maid's room or the
          other bedrooms had been occupied for a
          long time. But I saw some woman's
          clothing and other things in your
          bedroom.

                    MAX
          You're quite a sleuth, aren't you, Sadie
          Kupotel? By the way, what kind of name is
          that?

                    LINDA
          And you're a sleuth too, aren't you? I'm
          not sure, I just know I hate it.

A pause. Max rises abruptly.

                    MAX
          Something very important, don't invite
          anyone here. I can't have anyone coming
          here.

                    LINDA
          I won't. I don't have anyone to invite.

                    MAX
          For better or for worse, it's just the
          two of us.

He exits. She picks up her pencil and begins to write
furiously.

                    LINDA
          (Mouthing as she writes) For better or
          for worse, it's just the two of us.

BLACKOUT.

The End of Act I

ACT II

Lights up: The following afternoon. After a few moments,
Max and Linda enter. She is partially supporting him, her
arm around his waist, his hand on her shoulder. They stop
at his lounge chair.

                    LINDA (CONT'D)
          You sure you want to be out here?

                    MAX
          Yeah.

                    LINDA
          I think you may be more comfortable in
          bed.

                    MAX
          (Surly) You think? No, you're not
          thinking. If you were really thinking
          you'd think that I'm the best judge of
          where I'll be more comfortable.

                    LINDA
          All right.

She helps him into the lounge chair.

                    LINDA (CONT'D)
          Do you need anything?

                    MAX
          I feel a little chill. Get me a light
          blanket.

She enters the house. He turns his head and watches her
until she exits. He waits tensely until she returns with
a blanket. She covers him.

                    LINDA
          I have things to do inside. I'll keep
          checking on you. And if you call me, I'm
          sure I'll hear you.

                    MAX
          No. I want you out here. Get your
          notebook and sit at the round table. You
          can do your writing to occupy yourself. I
          want you close by.

                    LINDA
          All right.

She goes inside and returns in a moment with her writing
material.

                    LINDA (CONT'D)
          Do you want something to drink?

                    MAX
          No. Sit down. Don't interfere with me
          and I won't interfere with you.

She sits, opens her notebook. He is staring at her. It's
very awkward for her. They are both grim-faced. Finally,
she looks down at her notebook and begins to write.

He is still staring at her, she is aware of it. Finally,
she looks up.

                    LINDA
          I can't work this way.

                    MAX
          Why not? Who's bothering you?

                    LINDA
          You are.

                    MAX
          I didn't say a word.

                    LINDA
          It would probably be better if you did.

                    MAX
          My, my, aren't you creative artists
          touchy.

Furiously, she closes her notebook.

                    MAX (CONT'D)
          All right, I'm gonna close my eyes now
          and nap. You can't complain about that,
          can you?

He closes his eyes and lies very still. After a while,
she opens the notebook, finds her place and picks up her
pencil. She begins to write. Soon after, he opens his
eyes and begins to stare at her again. She becomes aware
that he is staring at her again. She throws down her
pencil in disgust.

                    LINDA
          I'm going inside.

                    MAX
I need you here.

                    LINDA
No, you don't.

                    MAX
I'll be the judge of that.

                    LINDA
You should have told me this was a twenty-
four hour a day job. The salary you're
paying doesn't seem so generous now.

                    MAX
Oh, I take it you want to open
negotiations now for a raise.

                    LINDA
Yes, why not? I won't be here very long.
I need to build up a nest egg in a hurry.

                    MAX
Your needs don't determine your worth as
an employee.

                    LINDA
Well, yours do.

                    MAX
Aha, you want to exploit my vulnerability
having just returned from a debilitating
treatment.

                    LINDA
Forget it.

                    MAX
No, no, there's some merit to your
position. Let's see, how much am I paying
you now?

                    LINDA
You know.

                    MAX
Oh, yes, four hundred. Well, suppose I
double that.

                    LINDA
Eight hundred dollars? You're not
serious.

> MAX
> When the subject is my money, I am always serious.

She doesn't know what to say.

> MAX (CONT'D)
> Well, is it a deal?

She nods yes.

> MAX (CONT'D)
> Good, that's a relief. Salary negotiations can be so taxing. Now help me relax by reading me something from your notebook.

> LINDA
> I can't do that.

> MAX
> Why not?

> LINDA
> It doesn't work for me.

> MAX
> Explain.

> LINDA
> That would open the door to... while I'm writing I don't want to be thinking about what someone else will be thinking about what I'm doing. It's like someone looking over my shoulder. I have to keep it to myself, a private matter. When the work is finished, that's a different matter.

> MAX
> Aha, you are explaining something about the creative process.

She's not quite sure if he's mocking her or being sincere.

> LINDA
> I suppose.

> MAX
> But since what you are writing is as much reportage as creative writing, and since I am the subject, why can't you make a small exception this time?

She is wavering.

                    MAX (CONT'D)
          Why not open your book at random and read
          something? Just a few minutes. I'll
          probably fall asleep, which will not be a
          commentary on your writing, just due to
          your soothing voice and the fact that I
          am very tired.

She surrenders, reaches for her notebook and opens it.

                    LINDA
          (Reading) My thoughts keep coming back to
          what Max told me about resigning his
          judgeship "under a cloud", as he put it.
          He seemed somewhat casual about his
          recital, and I detected something at the
          time that seemed inauthentic. The
          question, I think, is *why* did he confess
          this to me at all? He didn't have to. But
          of course, that's my point. He did, and
          he did not, spill his guts. With Max
          everything is a calculation. He is a
          complex man and nothing he says or does
          should necessarily be taken at face
          value. He is a proud man, that I am sure
          of. Was his confession then a test, to
          see if I cringed in horror at learning he
          was a corrupt man, or did he offer the
          information so blithely to convince
          himself that it was after all not such a
          big deal and that he barely transgressed
          "that amorphous line", as he referred to
          it. The truth, I am now convinced, is
          that the dark shadow of his disgrace
          hovers over him always and he is still
          coping with ways to deal with it. Of
          course, he needs to move on, but can he?

A long silence.

                    MAX
          You got it right. Also, I lied. I
          served two years in prison.

                    LINDA
          Then we have something in common. I have
          served time in jail-- an aggregate of at
          least three months in jail.

                    MAX
          (Forcing a mischievous smile) An
          aggregate?

                    LINDA
(With a slight smile)   An aggregate.

                    MAX
Linda, how much schooling have you had?

                    LINDA
Not much. I dropped out when I was
fifteen.

                    MAX
Then how did you get so smart?

                    LINDA
I spend a lot of time in libraries.
They're wonderful refuges. Warm in the
winter, cool in the summer. And all
those books. And so I thought I might as
well read some. And I read, and I read,
and I read.

                    MAX
Too bad you didn't pick one up on the
consequences of unprotected sex.

                    LINDA
Oh, I did read that one. I read novels,
too, and I knew this sort of thing could
happen to a young woman who falls in love
with the wrong guy.

                    MAX
And that happened to you?

                    LINDA
(Nods yes) All told I only knew him a
month. I knew he had a prison record. He
swore to me he was through with that. A
week later he was arrested while
committing a burglary. His third felony.
In California that means a mandatory life
sentence.

                    MAX
Does he know about your condition?

                    LINDA
No. We'll never be in contact again. He
didn't give a damn about me.

                    MAX
Are you seeing a doctor for prenatal
care?

                    LINDA
          No.

                    MAX
          What are you waiting for?

                    LINDA
          I'm healthy, there's no hurry.

                    MAX
          I don't think that's so smart.

                    LINDA
          Frankly, free clinics make me sick.

                    MAX
          (Studies her) I'll get a referral and
          arrange for private care.

                    LINDA
          Thanks.

                    MAX
          Sit there until I fall asleep. Then you
          can go swim. Or read a book. I've got
          books, too.

He closes his eyes and drops off to sleep.

BLACKOUT

Lights up: Afternoon, two days later. Linda and Max
enter. She is supporting him as in the previous scene,
but this time he appears to be weaker and more in need of
help.

                    MAX (CONT'D)
          It's never been this bad before.

                    LINDA
          You'll feel better as soon as you get
          settled.

She is struggling to keep him upright as they approach
his lounge chair. They trip over something and fall over
together, Max landing on top of her.

                    MAX
          Jesus Christ! Get me off the Goddamn
          floor!

                    LINDA
          You're on top of me. Move your legs.
          MOVE!

He changes his position. With difficulty, she struggles
to her feet.

                    MAX
          Goddammit, help get me to my feet! Don't
          let me lie here like a sack of potatoes!

She seems dazed. Nevertheless, she extends both hands and
helps pull him upright. He makes it to his lounge chair,
and reclines. She sits down in a chair.

                    LINDA
          (Stunned) Something happened. I felt
          something wrong. I don't want to lose my
          baby. I don't want to lose my baby. I
          don't want to lose my baby!

Max is alarmed. He struggles to his feet.

                    MAX
          Be calm, be calm. Don't move.

He makes his way to the corner bar and gets his cordless
phone. He punches in three numbers.

                    MAX (CONT'D)
          (Into phone) I need an ambulance.

BLACKOUT

Lights up: Six days later. Late in the evening, darkness
encroaching rapidly. Max is reclining in his usual place,
Linda is reclining in an identical lounge chair placed
parallel to and quite close to Max. Soft jazz is heard
from a cassette deck. After a while:

                    LINDA
          Do you want something?

                    MAX
          No, stay put.

                    LINDA
          I can start moving around.

                    MAX
          The doctor said to stay off your feet for
          a week. One more day to go.

                    LINDA
          I'm better, the spotting has ended. I
          know my body.

                    MAX
          It's a precaution.

                    LINDA
          I understand. I don't intend to break
          into a flamenco dance.

                    MAX
          Play it safe.

                    LINDA
          Thanks for your concern. (A beat) How are
          you doing?

                    MAX
          I'm not dead yet.

                    LINDA
          I noticed. (She begins to giggle) As a
          nurse, you leave a lot to be desired.

                    MAX
          You get what you pay for.

They fall silent.

                    LINDA
          Max, are you very, very rich?

                    MAX
          Filthy, filthy.

                    LINDA
          How did you make your money?

                    MAX
          I made it the old fashioned way, I stole
          it. But you already knew that, didn't
          you?

They fall silent. After a while:

                    LINDA
          Do you still miss Senora Ramirez?

A pause.

                    MAX
          Yes..

                    LINDA
          Was she attractive?

                    MAX
          Beautiful.

                    LINDA
          Oh.(A beat) What else?

                    MAX
          Huh?

                    LINDA
          What other qualities appealed to you?

                    MAX
          She had a lot of "qualities" that
          appealed to me.

                    LINDA
          (Encouraging) All right. Such as?

                    MAX
          Everything.

                    LINDA
          She was perfect.

                    MAX
          Damn near.

                    LINDA
          How old is she?

                    MAX
          Thirty-seven.

                    LINDA
          Gee.

     A Pause.

                    LINDA (CONT'D)
          Did you ever spend an evening out here
          with her like the two of us tonight?

                    MAX
          Frequently.

                    LINDA
          So, she was good company?

                    MAX
          Excellent company.

                    LINDA
          Then I guess she spoke English well. Or
          do you speak Spanish?

                    MAX
          Yes and yes.

                    LINDA
          Oh. What was her first name?

                    MAX
          Carmen.

                    LINDA
          (Laughs) Carmen?

She sings a bit in parody from Bizet's *Carmen*.

                    MAX
          Yes, Carmen.

                    LINDA
          Did you address her as Carmen?

                    MAX
          No, I always addressed her as Senora
          Ramirez, and she always addressed me as
          Senor Simon.

                    LINDA
          But you were lovers.

                    MAX
          Yes.

                    LINDA
          Did you address each other that way when
          you were in bed, making love?

                    MAX
          Exactly.

Linda is laughing.

                    MAX (CONT'D)
          Are you enjoying yourself?

                    LINDA
          (Still laughing) Yes, are you offended?

                    MAX
          No, not at all. I see the humor in it.
          Always have.
                    (MORE)

                    MAX (CONT'D)
As lovers we laughed at everything, at
ourselves, at each other, at what we were
doing. A word of advice, never have a
solemn lover, he'll bore the hell out of
you in all things.

                    LINDA
I'll certainly give your advice some
thought.

A long pause.

                    LINDA (CONT'D)
But if she returned to El Salvador due to
a family crises, why won't she return
when it's over?

                    MAX
I think she's ready to move on.

                    LINDA
How can you tell?

                    MAX
I helped her family out with a lot of
money. I sent money for her parents to
build a little villa, and then her
sisters and brothers and uncles and
cousins. I paid for enough homes to build
a complete village, for Christsake. I
hope they had the decency to name it
Simonville or some such thing.

                    LINDA
So are you saying she was just using you?

                    MAX
No, but she did what she had to do. She
has a couple of her own kids there and
probably a husband, too, although she was
a little vague about that.

                    LINDA
For such a hard-headed man, you are
really a believer in Senora Ramirez.

                    MAX
Yes, I know she really cared for me. For
her it was possible, she had an extra
dimension as a human being.

                    LINDA
What would you say if she contacted you
and said she was ready to return?

                    MAX
          I'd say yes, come, hurry.

A pause.

                    MAX (CONT'D)
          Well, have we exhausted the topic of
          Senora Ramirez?

She does not reply.

                    MAX (CONT'D)
          Too bad you didn't have your recorder on
          for this important revelation.

                    LINDA
          I didn't need it. It's all indelibly
          recorded in my brain.

                    MAX
          Then you have some pretty good material
          for your writing project?

                    LINDA
          Yes.

                    MAX
          See the kind of strange material you
          encounter when you start looking into
          someone's life?

                    LINDA
          Yes.

They are silent for a while. The music continues. She
reaches over to him and takes his hand briefly.

It is completely dark now. It is a beautiful night. A
long pause.

                    MAX
          Why do you insist on having a baby at
          this improbable time in your life?

                    LINDA
          I need the unconditional love of my baby.
          I need to give my baby my unconditional
          love. Or I'll die.

A long pause.

                        LINDA (CONT'D)
Max, I have something to tell you.
Senora Ramirez telephoned yesterday while
you were asleep. She wants you to call
her back. She said you have her number,
but she gave it to me again just in case.
I wasn't going to tell you, but obviously
I changed my mind.

He rises. For a while he just stands there staring down
at Linda. Suddenly, he turns away and exits.

BLACKOUT

Lights up: The following morning. Linda is standing on
the deck looking out in the direction of Catalina. After
a while, Max enters. Her back is to him and she is
unaware he is there until he speaks.

                    MAX
So, I take it Catalina's still there.

                    LINDA
(Half beat) Yes.

                    MAX
That's reassuring.

                    LINDA
Not for me. The thrill is gone. It's
just an inert, neutral blob.

                    MAX
Speaking on behalf of Catalina, "I've
never been so insulted in my life."

                    LINDA
Sorry, Catalina, you caught me on one of
those rare days when I just tell the
truth.

                    MAX
Come over here, Linda.

She turns. He indicates the round table. She comes over
and sits at the table. He sits at the table as well. They
are silent for a few moments.

                    LINDA
I can leave as early as today if that's
you want.

A pause. He appears to be considering what she said.

>   MAX
>   I called her back last night. The reason
>   she called was to ask me to send her the
>   things she left behind.

>   LINDA
>   She's not coming back?

>   MAX
>   No.

>   LINDA
>   Are you very disappointed?

>   MAX
>   Strangely, no.

>   LINDA
>   That's a lot different than what you said
>   last night.

>   MAX
>   (Shrugs) Yes.

>   LINDA
>   You're confusing me.

>   MAX
>   I've told you many times I'm not an easy
>   man to figure out. Even with my vaunted
>   analytical power, I've never succeeded.

>   LINDA
>   I'll pack her things.

>   MAX
>   I was hoping you'd volunteer.

She starts to get up, he restrains her.

>   MAX (CONT'D)
>   You might be interested to know I was
>   seriously depressed when she came here.
>   She was my servant, my nurse, my mother,
>   my companion, my mistress. Highly skilled
>   in all those areas, and also she had a
>   sly and engaging sense of humor. Twice a
>   year, I would send her off to El Salvador
>   to be with her family for a while.

                              MAX (CONT'D)
          This "arrangement" went on for seven
          years. Oh, the things money can buy. When
          she left, my depression began to return
          until one fine day I met one Linda
          Lane... Sadie Kupotel. Stick around,
          please, as long as you can put up with
          me. I hope you can stay the course.. I
          won't be around that much longer.

                              LINDA
          I don't like you to talk that way.

                              MAX
          What the hell. (A beat) What I have just
          said so clumsily is I really want you to
          stay.

                              LINDA
          You're not afraid I might murder you in
          your sleep?

                              MAX
          I'll take my chances.

                              LINDA
          Maybe you ought to rethink your
          invitation. As you already know, I come
          with a certain amount of baggage.

He shrugs indeterminately.

                              LINDA (CONT'D)
          My grandmother was still a young woman
          when she took me to live with her. She
          was a devout Christian and she recognized
          she had a duty to take me in. But that
          was the end of her Christian charity. She
          hated and resented her burden and she
          never ran out of ways to let me know. I
          can't remember a single instance of love
          or affection. Abuse was her stock in
          trade. I was fifteen when I left. I've
          been a drug addict, alcoholic,
          prostitute, petty thief, shoplifter and
          grifter. So understandably, Max, I am
          tired now. I am so very tired. (She
          breaks down) I *am so fucking tired.*

He embraces her. Sobbing, she buries her head in his
chest.

BLACKOUT

Lights up: The same day. A lovely star-studded night. Max and Linda are in their side by side lounge chairs. Soft music.

>   LINDA (CONT'D)
>   I imagine this is something like being
>   out on the deck of a cruise ship at
>   night.

>   MAX
>   Somewhat.

>   LINDA
>   I've never been on a cruise ship.
>   (she laughs)
>   I'm sure that comes as a big surprise.
>   I've never been on a ship of any kind.
>   I've never been on a plane.

>   MAX
>   The pleasure of travel is over-rated. The
>   best part of any trip is returning home.

>   LINDA
>   Maybe I can believe that, if it's a home
>   like this.

>   MAX
>   So, you like my home.

>   LINDA
>   Ah, ah.

>   MAX
>   I'll take that as a yes.

>   LINDA
>   Yes, a gigantic yes.

>   MAX
>   Very well, it's yours.

>   LINDA
>   What's mine?

>   MAX
>   The house. I just gave it to you.

>   LINDA
>   (playing along)
>   Oh, thank you very much.

>   MAX
>   You're welcome.

A long pause.

                    LINDA
          Is that binding?

                    MAX
               (almost asleep)
          What?

                    LINDA
          The gift of your house?

                    MAX
          No. It's got to be in writing.

                    LINDA
          Oh, damn legal technicalities.

                    MAX
          Don't worry, I'll do it right tomorrow.
          Just pray that I survive the night.

                    LINDA
          Max, I don't like it when you talk that
          way.

                    MAX
          All right. Actually, I've been feeling
          pretty good for a while.

                    LINDA
          I know it gets very bad at times.

                    MAX
          After the treatments. The rest of the
          time, the medications work well.

                    LINDA
          Maybe they'll find a cure. Or you'll turn
          out to be an aberration.

                    MAX
               (laughing))
          An aberration?

                    LINDA
          Did I say something wrong?

                    MAX
          No, you said something right.

                    LINDA
          Are you afraid?

                    MAX
Not so much. What I am is embarrassed,
humiliated.

                    LINDA
Why?

                    MAX
The attention I'm getting is not the
attention I crave. Even when the
caregivers are being gentle and kind, I
know I'm just a unit on a conveyor belt
being poked and sliced and probed on the
way to the final exit. The paradox is I'm
getting all this high tech care and yet I
never felt so insignificant.

A pause.

                    MAX (CONT'D)
          (jocular)
You going to put that in your story about
me?

                    LINDA
Yes, without much editing I imagine.

                    MAX
I don't want to tell you how to work, but
if you put it in quotation marks, they'll
know it's my voice.

                    LINDA
I won't change it much.

He waves in acknowledgment. A pause.

                    MAX
They say a dying man sees his entire life
flash before him. I guess I haven't
reached that stage yet, but what I'm
experiencing is quite interesting. I'm
experiencing very early sensations in my
life, not memories... *sensations.* Call
them inchoate memories, if you will. I
recall my innocence, my sense of wonder
and awe, my excitement and fright and
eagerness about the world, and my life
poised to unfold. That's the only part of
myself I feel any affection for.
          (a beat)
It's too bad you haven't got your
recorder on.

                    LINDA
          You banned it.

                    MAX
          Maybe I'll have to rethink that.

Max sits up, turns to face Linda.

                    MAX (CONT'D)
          I meant it about the house. The idea
          you'll be remaining here thrills me. Yes,
          live here, and if you want to be a
          mother, be a mother. If you want to be a
          writer, be a writer. You can do it. I
          knew you were a very special person the
          moment you started talking to me at
          Starbucks. I felt strongly drawn to you.

                    LINDA
          Max, this is coming at me so fast I don't
          know what to think, let alone what to
          say.

                    MAX
          Oh, my, are you going to let me go on
          dominating the conversation?

                    LINDA
          You usually do. And I love what I'm
          hearing so please continue.

                    MAX
          But now for the bad news, there are
          conditions to my gift. Sorry, but in the
          real world, as you know, there are always
          conditions.

                    LINDA
          Uh, uh.

                    MAX
          Let's go over to the rail and let
          Catalina witness this. Unless you still
          feel it's an inert, neutral blob.

He leads her to the rail.

                    LINDA
          You remember everything I say.

                    MAX
          Yes, and you still owe me a meal at
          McDonalds.

They are looking out now.

                    MAX (CONT'D)
          I want you to name your child Max.

                    LINDA
          Okay, but suppose it's a girl.

                    MAX
          Max. Put Maxine on the birth certificate
          if you must, but call her Max.

                    LINDA
          All right. I agree.

                    MAX
          Not so fast. There's still the matter of
          the second name. I want it to be Simon.

Linda is stunned.

                    MAX (CONT'D)
          There are a number of reasons. Let me
          explain. My former wives are completely
          excluded from my estate, but as often
          happens with a big estate there are
          distant relatives that come out of the
          woodwork and make a claim. You'll be in
          the strongest possible position if we are
          married and especially if the baby is
          born after we marry.

Linda is about to speak, but Max stops her.

                    MAX (CONT'D)
          Also, I have to tell you, I love the idea
          of having a child bear my name.

                    LINDA
          You said you hated children.

                    MAX
          I changed my mind.

                    LINDA
          Have you told me all the reasons?

                    MAX
          No.

He hugs her, places a kiss on her forehead.

                    LINDA
          I couldn't consider living with a man who
          can always tell when I'm lying. What is
          it I do that gives me away?

                    MAX
          Nothing. You're a superb liar. I was
          lying. But tonight everything I said was
          the truth.

                    LINDA
          Max, you're my Prince Charming.

                    MAX
          Prince Charming. And my parents said I
          would never amount to anything.

A long pause. They are looking out.

                    LINDA
          It's so beautiful. I've made my peace
          with Catalina. And look, the sky is
          loaded with stars.

                    MAX
          Does this qualify as savoring the moment
          with someone special?

                    LINDA
          Yes, it does. And for you?

                    MAX
          Yes.

They are looking out.

BLACKOUT

Staged reading at The Motion Picture and Television Fund with Marvin Kaplan. Reading at The Village at Northridge with Max Gail.

JULES AND JAKE
A play in two acts
An homage to Francois Truffaut

Cast of Characters

Narrator's Voice,

Jules, late 70s

Jake, late 70s

Jenny, mid 60s

Gert, middle aged

Mr. Greenblatt, 80

The Rabbi, in his 60s

Setting:

The grounds of The Golden Years Leisure Living retirement home, Los Angeles, California

Park bench at the retirement home

Park bench in Santa Monica

The cafeteria

The recreation room

A hospital waiting room

Rabbi's office

All scenes to be represented minimally.

The attractive grounds of Golden Years Leisure Living, an upscale retirement home for Jewish seniors.

Jules, about seventy-five, is sitting on a bench, reading a newspaper. His face is obscured by the pages of the paper he is holding up.

After a moment, he turns the page without lowering the paper. Jake, about seventy-five, approaches. He plops down on the same bench. We hear the Narrator's Voice, a rather soft, gently ironic voice as it floats from the ether.

We never see the NARRATOR. It is only a voice.

                    NARRATOR
          What you are witnessing is two friends,
          Jules and Jake, start their day more or
          less the same way they do most days. But
          after that, each day brings it's unique
          characteristics, or it should anyway. But
          there are not many variations for Jules
          and Jake. They live in a retirement home -
          not that much going on. Perhaps that's
          what we all do, all our lives. No, that
          can't be true. Anyway, I'm just the
          unseen narrator and it's not my place to
          wax philosophical.

                    JAKE
          What's the news of the day?

                    JULES
          Same old, same old.

                    JAKE
          I dreamt about you last night.

                    JULES
          I'm honored.

                    JAKE
          Also, I had an erection in the middle of
          the night.

Jules lowers his newspaper, fixes a stern look on Jake.

                    JULES
          I don't think I want to discuss this.

                    JAKE
          Relax, you were not the object of my
          affection.

                    JULES
          Thank heaven.

He raises the paper again.

                    JAKE
          Let's get breakfast.

                    JULES
          Let's wait.

                    JAKE
          You continue with the news, it will only
          ruin your digestion.

                    JULES
          It's already ruined.

                    JAKE
          I want to tell you about an amazing
          experience I had last night.

                    JULES
               (accusingly)
          You already did, didn't you?

                    JAKE
          Well, no, not exactly. You'll never
          guess what happened.

                    JULES
          Now you are repelling me and piquing my
          interest at the same time.

He lowers his newspaper and gestures to Jake to continue.

                    JAKE
          I fell in love.

                    JULES
          Oh....that's nice.

He returns to his newspaper.

                    JAKE
          Jules, listen, I'm not kidding. This is
          serious.

                    JULES
               (his face still in his paper)
          Serious? Perhaps. But I have to tell
          you, in all honesty, I don't rate it as
          high as war and peace and the state of
          the economy.

He turns the page again without lowering the paper.

                    JAKE
          Then I have to tell you, you got your
          priorities wrong.

                    JULES
          Maybe.

A pause.

Jake gives up.

                    JAKE
          All right, where do you want to go for
          lunch today?

                    JULES
          Lunch? We haven't had breakfast yet.

                    JAKE
          What's wrong with a little advance
          planning?

                    JULES
          You say you like the food here so much,
          so why go out?

                    JAKE
          Come on, Jules, we need a little variety,
          a little excitement in our lives.

                    JULES
          Going out to Denny's for lunch is
          excitement?

                    JAKE
          We'll go to the beach. I'll drive.

                    JULES
          Now that, I grant you, is exciting,
          because driving with you is also life
          threatening.

                    JAKE
          You exaggerate. I still have one good
          eye. And my coordination - like a
          teenager.

                    JULES
          The only thing you have in common with a
          teenager is recklessness. And maybe
          horniness.

                    JAKE
          Then you drive.

                         JULES
          I know my limitations.

Jenny, in a jogging outfit, runs by them on the path
right in front of their bench. She is about sixty-five.
She waves as she goes by with just a fleeting glance at
them.

                         JENNY
                    (with a lilt in her voice)
          Good morning.

She does not break her stride. A beat.

                         JAKE
                    (excited)
          That's her, that's her!

                         JULES
          That's who?

                         JAKE
          The woman I started to tell you about.
          The one I fell in love with.

                         JULES
                    (watching Jenny run down the
                     path)
          Then it appears to be unrequited love.
          In fact, I think she was looking at me
          when she said good morning.

                         JAKE
                    (disconsolate)
          I don't think she recognized me. She's
          beautiful.

                         JULES
                    (looking down the path)
          Her tush isn't bad.

                         JAKE
          Be careful how you talk about the woman I
          love.

                         JULES
          Pardon me. And why don't you tell me now
          how you met her and made such an
          indelible impression.

                         JAKE
          She's my new neighbor. She moved into
          the room next door to mine. We share the
          same landing.

                    JULES
          So, you called on her with a welcome
          basket?

                    JAKE
          Very funny. Listen, the first time I
          laid eyes on her was last night. She was
          trying to open the door to her room. She
          had a bunch of packages in both arms and
          somehow she was trying to turn the key in
          her lock. But the top parcel fell to the
          ground as I was passing. So, I picked it
          up and as I was about to restore it to
          the top of the mountain of packages, our
          eyes met. You see, we were then standing
          face to face...

                    JULES
          Yes, that figures.

                    JAKE
          She has blue eyes. The most gorgeous
          eyes I've seen in my life. I put the
          parcel back on top and she didn't say a
          word, she just smiled. The most
          beautiful smile I've seen in my life.
          Somehow she managed to open the door and
          go inside kicking it shut with the back
          of her foot. But that smile, it didn't
          go away. It had an afterglow, a positive
          afterglow. I went inside my room and I
          looked at my TV without turning it on.
          The afterglow of her smile was there. It
          made me incredibly happy just to keep
          looking at it. I went to sleep with that
          afterglow in my mind's eye.

                    JULES
          Yet you told me you dreamt of me last
          night. How come?

                    JAKE
          I don't know what you were doing there.
          You were an intruder. Don't ever do it
          again.

                    JULES
          I'll do my best to stay away. But
          nobody's perfect.

                    JAKE
          Let's get breakfast.

     They rise.

                         JAKE (CONT'D)
                    (suddenly happy, sings)
          I'm in love, I'm in love with a beautiful
          girl...

They are standing face to face. Jake does a little gig.
Jules clasps Jake's shoulder.

                         JULES
          My dear friend, I'm sorry to tell you,
          that aint no girl and you aint no boy.

Jake clasps Jules' shoulder.

                         JAKE
          My dear friend, I'm happy to tell you,
          you are wrong.
                    (half beat)
          Your grammar sucks too. Let's go. I'm
          starving.

The lights adjust as the scene shifts to a small section
of the dining room at Golden Years Leisure Living. A
brief musical bridge, a ballad from the 1930s plays.

Jake and Jules enter and sit down at a small table.
Almost immediately, the waitress, Gert, approaches.

                         GERT
          Good morning, gentlemen.

                         JAKE
          Gentlemen? She forgets us from day to
          day.

                         GERT
          That's not so easy, but I'm working on
          it.
                    (to Jules)
          The usual?

He nods yes, Gert writes on her pad

                         GERT (CONT'D)
          A dish of stewed prunes, a bowl of
          oatmeal, whole wheat toast, no butter,
          decaf black.
                    (to Jake)
          You are not so predictable, but I can be
          sure your order will be nothing like
          that.
                    (half beat, pencil poised)
          I'm waiting.

                    JAKE
          First, give me a sweet smile. Come on.
                    (she makes a funny face)
          That's it. More, more. Stop, I don't
          want to get diabetes.

                    GERT
          Okay, we've done our little shtick, now
          what can I get you?

                    JAKE
          An omelet made with three eggs - no
          cheating, with avocado, jack cheese and
          home fried potatoes. White toast, lots
          of butter, regular coffee with cream.

                    GERT
          Skipping the sausage today?

                    JAKE
          Yeah, I'm dieting. Doctor's orders.

Gert exits

                    JAKE (CONT'D)
          So, when does your daily lecture on the
          evils of fat and cholesterol begin? I'm
          waiting.

                    JULES
          Not today. Maybe never again. Observing
          you place your order today I think I had
          a breakthrough in understanding what's
          going on.

                    JAKE
          Really? And the breakthrough is?

                    JULES
          First, the question is why would a guy
          who has already had two bypass surgeries
          do exactly the opposite of what the
          doctors say he should do. And the answer
          is: it is a clear act of defiance. A
          defiance so perverse it's almost
          admirable.

                    JAKE
          That was a little hard for me to follow.
          But, from what I do understand, I think
          you got it wrong.

                    JULES
          So, how do you explain it?

                         JAKE
          It's very simple. I listen to what you
          order and I think to myself, this must
          never happen to me.

                         JULES
                    (hurt)
          That's not very flattering.

                         JAKE
                    (not sorry)
          Sorry.

                         JULES
          All right, next time you order first and
          maybe you'll use better judgment. My
          problem is I've gotten used to having you
          around so I'm being selfish about this.

A pause.

Jake is silent but he is moved by his friend's concern.

Gert brings the coffee.

                         GERT
          Decaf here.
                    (she serves Jules)
          Regular here.
                    (she serves Jake. To Jake)
          Your order will take a while. When I
          told the chef it was for you he said he
          would have to send out for more eggs,
          cheese and butter.

                         JAKE
          Tell him I'll settle for two eggs, skip
          the cheese and potatoes and substitute
          sliced tomatoes and whole wheat bread.

                         GERT
          That's interesting. You mean it?

                         JAKE
          I'm turning over a new leaf because my
          friend here loves me.

                         GERT
                    (to Jules)
          Do you love him?

                         JULES
          No comment.

Gert exits. Jake leans in to Jules' face, puckers up and kisses the air continuously.

Jules begins to crack-up.

                    JULES (CONT'D)
               (going along)
          Stop it. People will talk.

                    JAKE
          I don't care what people say.
               (looks about the room)
          Anyhow, there's no one here except...
               (his eyes light up)
          Excuse me...
               (he gets up suddenly almost
                knocking his chair over)
          I shall return.

He is back in a moment, his arm linked through Jenny's.

They are laughing.

                    JAKE (CONT'D)
          I told this newcomer we are on the
          welcoming committee here and she is
          required to join us for breakfast.

                    JENNY
               (laughing)
          I always follow the rules...well, some of
          the time.

Jules rises. They are all standing now.

                    JAKE
          Time for the introductions. I am Jake
          Rosenberg, this is my best friend, Jules
          Rubin. And, you are?...

                    JENNY
          I am Jenny Rosen.

She extends her hand to Jake and they shake and to Jules and they shake hands.

Jake grabs a chair from another table, positions it and they all sit.

                    JENNY (CONT'D)
          You know, this is uncanny. It really is.

                    JULES
          What's uncanny?

> JENNY
> Our names. Didn't you notice our first
> names all start with "J" and our second
> names with "R" and they are similar
> names. There must be a reason for that.

> JULES
> What sort of reason?

> JENNY
> Everything happens for a reason,
> everything has meaning.

> JULES
> What's the meaning?

> JENNY
> It will be revealed.

> JULES
> It will?

Jenny lightly clasps Jules' wrist.

> JENNY
> Oh, Jules, I don't think you're a very
> spiritual man.

> JULES
> Right, I've never been accused of that.

Jake lightly clasps Jenny's free wrist.

> JAKE
> Hey, I'm spiritual. I'm very spiritual.

Jenny smiles at him. Jake is beaming.

A beat.

> JENNY
> I think I know. The meaning is we three
> are fated to be very close friends.

They are happy.

The scene shifts to a park bench at the Pacific Palisades
in Santa Monica, overlooking the ocean. Musical bridge
is heard.

It is afternoon on a sunny, balmy day. The sound of
laughter is heard as Jenny, Jake and Jules approach and
sit, Jenny in the middle.

They look out at the ocean.

                    JENNY (CONT'D)
          I love the ocean. This is so beautiful!

                    JAKE
          It's great!

                    JULES
          It's nice.

                    JENNY
          Oh, look at the squirrel. It's so cute.

She is looking down at a little mound, partially obscured
by brush, off to the side in front of the bench.

                    JAKE
          That fellow's really looking us over.

                    JULES
          It can't be more than three feet away.
          Undoubtedly, it's used to having people
          close by.

                    JENNY
          Uh, uh, he ducked into his hole.

                    JAKE
          There, he's popped out again for another
          look. He's sure giving us the once over.
          I wonder what he's thinking? Maybe, who
          is that old geezer and that great looking
          mature man and that beautiful, mature
          woman?

                    JULES
          If you're nominating me for the role of
          old geezer, I would remind you I'm
          younger than you are.

                    JAKE
          Hey, I'm not talking chronological age
          here.

                    JENNY
          Now, fellows, in my eyes you're both...
                    (she gives them both the once
                     over)
          ...Incredibly good looking soon to be but
          not quite yet...old geezers.

All laugh. She looks in the direction of the squirrel
again.

                    JENNY (CONT'D)
          Oh, I wish I had some peanuts for him.

                    JAKE
               (jumps to feet)
          Peanuts? You want peanuts, I'll get
          peanuts.

                    JULES
          Hey, where do you think you are, the
          ballpark with peanut vendors all over the
          place?

                    JAKE
          I'll go down to the pier, they sell
          peanuts at those food stands.

                    JULES
          Yeah, that's quite a hike.

                    JAKE
          What are you talking about?
               (pointing)
          The pier is right there.

                    JULES
          It's easy getting down there, but maybe
          you forgot that's a long, steep incline
          getting back to this level.

                    JAKE
          It's nothing.

                    JULES
               (on his feet, to Jenny)
          I can get them in no time.

                    JENNY
          Oh, sit down, both of you.

They sit.

There is some discernible tension between the men.

                    JENNY (CONT'D)
               (looking down to the
                squirrel)
          There, he's bored with us, he went away.
               (a beat)
          Oh, you know what Mrs. Needleman told me
          this morning? She said people have
          started referring to us as the three
          musketeers. And, you know the motto of
          the three musketeers. All for one...
               (MORE)

                    JENNY (CONT'D)
                (she prompts them and they
                 join in)

                    ALL
          ...And one for all.

They laugh. A pause. They look out, enjoy the ocean
view and the camaraderie.

                    JAKE
          Damn, this is great!

                    JULES
          It really is enjoyable.

Jenny is smiling contentedly.

                    JULES (CONT'D)
                (spontaneously, to Jenny))
          You've got a wonderful smile.

Jake shoots him a look.

Jenny removes a little note pad from her purse.

                    JENNY
          Thank you. I've jotted down some places
          I think we should visit in the coming
          days. Let me know what you think.
          Olvera Street, I haven't been there in
          years and I lust for the wonderful
          tamales you can get there.

                    JAKE
          Sounds wonderful.

                    JULES
          Good.

                    JENNY
          The Farmers Market.

                    JAKE
          Terrific choice. I used to go there all
          the time.

                    JULES
                (nods approval)
          And I've read about this attractive, new
          entertainment and shopping center they've
          added on. Something else to explore.

                    JENNY
And in that neighborhood, there's also
the Los Angeles County Museum.

                    JAKE
          (not enthusiastic)
Museum?

                    JULES
Good.

                    JENNY
          (picking up on Jake's
          displeasure)
All right, let's eliminate that for the
present and substitute The Getty Museum,
which really should be on the top of our
list in any case.
          (to Jake)
Even if you don't care for the exhibits
I'm sure you'll enjoy the architecture
and the view and the lovely garden.

                    JAKE
Do they have a restaurant?

                    JENNY
More than one.

                    JAKE
Count me in.

                    JENNY
Well, I can go on and on. And, of
course, I'm open to suggestions.

                    JAKE
I suggest that whatever we do together
we'll have a great time.

                    JULES
I agree.

                    JULES (CONT'D)
          (a beat)
I also think, Jenny, the time has come
for you to tell us the story of your life
or at least some highlights. In a way,
you're quite a mystery woman.

                    JENNY
          (laughs)
My life is an open book. I mean that
literally. I was a librarian.

                    JAKE
A librarian. Somehow you're not the
type.

                    JENNY
You're right, I sure didn't fit the
stereotype. Instead of being a spinster
type, I was married three times. I
didn't wear glasses, I wasn't sedate.
Instead of shushing the people in the
library for making too much noise, I had
to shush myself. But, I do love books.

                    JULES
Can we get back to the "I was married
three times" statement, that is, if you
care to discuss it?

                    JENNY
Why not? The first time was a disaster,
the mistake of a very rash young woman.
The only good thing about it, it didn't
last long. The other marriages - both my
husbands died too young, were wonderful.

                    JAKE
Children?

                    JENNY
No children.
        (a beat)
Now what about you fellows? You haven't
volunteered that much about your lives.
I do hear rumors about you though, and
they're pretty wild.

                    JAKE
Rumors? What rumors?

                    JENNY
Okay, Jake, I'll start with you.

                    JENNY (CONT'D)
I heard you were married five times, have
a total of thirteen children and twenty-
five grandchildren. And that you owned
the largest fashion shoe factory in
America.

                    JAKE
Substantially true. A few errors in
arithmetic of no great consequence.

                    JENNY
Well, all right. And you, Jules, they
say you were an important official in the
CIA and that's why, to this day, you are
very secretive even about your personal
life.

                    JULES
And that being the case, of course I
can't comment on it.

                    JENNY
          (laughing)
You fellows are too much.

                    JULES
Well, we have provided a little
disinformation to our fellow residents at
good old Golden Years Leisure Living.

                    JENNY
But why?

                    JULES
We live in an environment where people
can latch onto you and be real pests. It
can be big problem. We have found that
being ridiculous, insincere and sometimes
downright rude can keep them at bay.
Being subtle doesn't cut it.

                    JENNY
Well, I guess it can be difficult to
maintain your privacy at times.

A homeless man, laden with all his personal belongings,
walks by on the path in front of the bench.

                    JENNY (CONT'D)
There are so many homeless people here.

                    JAKE
Yeah, they call Santa Monica the home of
the homeless.

                    JULES
There are too many everywhere in our
country. It's a failure of our society.
We spend too much time congratulating
ourselves while ignoring festering
problems.

                        JAKE
                (to Jenny)
        Uh, uh, don't let him get on his soap
        box. He not only spends hours reading
        the papers, he actually writes letters to
        the editor.

                        JENNY
        He's right, of course.
                (trying to introduce levity)
        But, frankly I didn't expect such
        outspokenness from anyone associated with
        the CIA.

                        JULES
                (impressed)
        Not that I mind, but, I thought you'd be
        more likely to talk about horoscopes and
        things of that nature.

                        JENNY
        I love horoscopes. What's your sign?
        I'm an Aquarius.

                        JAKE
        Cancer.

                        JULES
        Leo.

                        JENNY
        Okay, I have some horoscope material in
        my room and from time to time I'll keep
        you informed.

They look out to the sea. Simultaneously, she touches
the wrist of each man. They are happy. Lights dim.

Morning. Jules is alone on his regular bench reading his
paper, arms outstretched, the paper in front of his face.
Jake approaches, stops and stands looking down at Jules.

                        JULES
        Did I hear the pitter patter of little
        feet approach?

                        JAKE
        Listen, Jules, I want to talk to you.

                        JULES
                (taken aback, lowers his
                 paper)
        Good morning.

Jake sits down.

                    JAKE
          I want to ask you something.

                    JULES
          Okay.

                    JAKE
          I want to know how you feel about Jenny.

                    JULES
          Oh, you want to talk about my feelings?

                    JAKE
          You know what I mean?

                    JULES
          I'm not so sure I do. But, on the other
          hand, I may have an idea.

                    JAKE
          Then why don't you answer my question.

                    JULES
          Maybe I don't like its tone, it sounds a
          tad inquisitorial?

                    JAKE
          No matter what you answer, you will not
          be burned at the stake.

                    JULES
          Okay, then.
               (a beat)
          Look, Jake, I like her, I like her a lot.
          She's fun. She's a nice person. She
          helps brighten my day. And I have no
          reservations about admitting her to that
          select club that previously had the
          exclusive membership of Jules and Jake.

                    JAKE
          You don't have a romantic interest in
          her?

                    JULES
          I believe my days for having a romantic
          interest in anyone are over.

                    JAKE
          Mine aren't.

They fall silent.

                    JAKE (CONT'D)
          I didn't think I'd ever feel this way
          again about a woman. But, I do. I
          wanted you to know.

                    JULES
          Okay.

A pause.

                    JAKE
          Thanks.

                    JULES
          Why are you thanking me?

Jake makes an indeterminate gesture. A pause.

                    JAKE
          I enjoy it a lot when the three of us go
          places together. I want it to continue.
          But, I'd also like some time with her
          alone.

                    JULES
          That's up to the two of you, isn't it?
          I'm not your rival, Jake.

                    JAKE
          I'm a little embarrassed by this. But, I
          had to get it off my chest.

Jenny in her running clothes, jogs by. Without breaking
her stride, she calls:

                    JENNY
          Good morning, Jules, good morning, Jake.

They watch her recede, then look at each other. They
begin to laugh. Lights dim.

Lights up. Their table in the dining room - Jules and
Jake enter and sit at their customary places.

                    JAKE
          Should we wait for Jenny before we order?

                    JULES
          If Gert gets here first, we can order.
          Jenny won't mind, she never eats anything
          substantial for breakfast.

Gert appears at their table.

                    GERT
Ready now or do you want to wait for
Jenny?

                    JAKE
Now isn't that interesting, we just had a
little powwow on that very subject and
decided we wouldn't wait.

                    GERT
Doesn't matter, all she orders is a bagel
or toast. So what will it be?

                    JAKE
I'll have a bowl of oatmeal, and a dish
of stewed prunes.

                    GERT
Hey, you're really sticking to your
healthy diet.

                    JAKE
Of course. I've come to enjoy a hearty
bowl of oatmeal. It's nutritious and it
sticks to the ribs - whatever that means.
And stewed prunes, listen if it weren't
for the senior citizens of the world the
entire prune industry would go down the
toilet.

                    JULES
No pun was intended, I'm sure, but very
apt. I'll have the usual.

Jenny approaches, sits.

                    JENNY
Good morning, Gert. These fellows I've
already seen this morning, sitting on the
bench engrossed in a serious
conversation.

                    GERT
Serious?
        (looks at Jake)
I think you only got half of that right
as far as this one is concerned. What
can I get you?

                    JENNY
I'll have a plain bagel and a small
orange juice.

                    GERT
          Want the bagel toasted?

                    JENNY
          Okay.

                    GERT
          Butter or cream cheese?

                    JAKE
          Tell her both even if you don't want the
          cream cheese. I'll eat it.

Gert wags her finger at Jake.

                    GERT
          Uh, uh, uh....

                    JENNY
               (to Gert)
          Okay, both.

Gert gives Jake a dirty look and exits.

                    JAKE
          You know that woman is very fond of me.

                    JULES
          I don't want to feed your ego but you're
          probably right.

                    JAKE
          What can I say? It was ever thus.

                    JENNY
          Have you written your memoirs yet? It
          should be a good read.

                    JAKE
               (heartfelt)
          Not yet, because I hope and pray the best
          is yet to come.

                    JENNY
          Good luck.
               (a beat)
          Are you fellows free to go on a little
          outing today?

                    JAKE
          Absolutely.

                    JULES
I think I'll have to take a rain check
today.

                    JENNY
Oh?

                    JAKE
I've got an idea, a great idea for the
two of us. Why didn't I think of this
before? It takes a little explaining.
You may laugh at me when I tell you.

                    JENNY
I'm a decent person, I'll restrain my
laughter.

                    JAKE
Okay, you know I was in the shoe
business.

                    JENNY
Oh, yes, the largest manufacturer of high
fashion shoes in the country.

                    JAKE
Well, not exactly. Actually, I was a
factory representative. I represented
some of the finest lines in the Country.
And especially in the old days, before
the giant chains swallowed up everything,
I called on high fashion department
stores and small chains of high fashion
foot wear. I introduced the owners and
the buyers to the new styles, solved
problems, pampered them, humored them and
entertained them in nightclubs and fine
restaurants, on a generous expense
account of course. It was great. I
loved my work, I loved the shoe business,
I loved shoes. And now finally, I'm
coming to the point.

                    JENNY
It's so nice when a man loves his work.

                    JULES
It's also nice when he comes to the
point.

                    JAKE
So, here's what I'm getting to. I began
to keep for myself one or two pairs of my
favorite new styles when they came out.
                    (MORE)

JAKE (CONT'D)
I'm not talking about shoes I got for my
wife and daughters, these were for my
private collection.

JENNY
You kept the samples?

JAKE
No, samples are sized too small for most
women. I kept size six, only size six.

JULES
Did you have a shoe fetish, or something?

JAKE
No, a man can be a little eccentric,
without being a meshugenna.

JULES
That judgment is in the eye of the
beholder.

JAKE
So, Mr. Smart guy, let me finish.

JULES
    (assumed innocence)
Have I been the real impediment to
getting this story finished?

JENNY
    (gently reproving)
Oh, come on, Jules.

JULES
Then just one question, if I may, why
size six?

JAKE
All right, that's a good question. Six
is my favorite size, most beautiful
women, in my opinion, are size six. Take
Jenny here, for example, she's size six.

JENNY
I am a six, how did you know?

JAKE
    (proudly)
How did I know? First, I look at a
woman's beautiful face and I already have
an idea. Then, just a glimpse of her
feet and I know. I'm never wrong.

                         JULES
          Well, every man should excel at
          something.

                         JAKE
          Now for the kicker.

Jules is about to speak.

                         JENNY
                  (firmly to Jules)
          Jules, don't interrupt.

                         JULES
          See, he's won you over by talking about
          your feet.

They all laugh.

                         JAKE
          Okay, I had this really large collection
          of shoes accumulated over the years.
          When I had my own home, storage was not a
          problem. When I moved here, I couldn't
          bring them here and I couldn't bring
          myself to get rid of my collection, so I
          rented a storage space. I never go
          there, I get my monthly storage bill and
          I write a check. It's silly, I suppose,
          it's certainly a waste of money, but
          there it is.
                  (Jake rises)
          And now, dear lady, I wish to make you,
          Jenny Rosen, the official beneficiary of
          any and all of my shoe collection. As
          you wish. And for today's activity,
          let's go visit my...your collection.

                         JENNY
          I'm flabbergasted, truly flabbergasted.

Gert approaches with the food as Jake sits down.

                         GERT
          What's going on here?

                         JULES
          Gert, what's your shoe size?

                         GERT
          I consider that a personal question, but
          I'll answer anyway. I was a seven narrow
          when I started to work here. I'm a ten
          wide now.

                    JULES
Too bad. If you were a six you might
have been eligible for a free pair of
high fashion shoes. Sorry, you're out of
luck.

                    GERT
Yeah, the story of my life.

She completes serving the food and exits.

                    JENNY
Jake, this is exciting. But in a way,
it's kind of ironic, because I rarely
wear shoes anymore.

Jenny turns in her chair and extends a leg

                    JENNY (CONT'D)
I'm afraid I've turned out to be one of
these older women who wear tennis shoes
most of the time.

                    JAKE
I see. Well, there's always the
occasional wedding or bar mitzvah you
might want to dress up for.

                    JULES
More likely funerals.

                    JENNY
Jake, I'll tell you what I'd like to do
with the shoes. I do volunteer work for
an organization that raises money for
cancer research. They operate a chain of
used clothing stores. Very nice
merchandise, obviously donated by people
who are well off. And they also get
donations from time to time of new
things. Would you be willing to donate
your shoes?

                    JAKE
Of course. But we're going to the
storage place today.

                    JENNY
Sure.
        (to Jules)
Can't you come, too?

                    JULES
Not today.

They start to eat.

As the lights dim on this area, we hear the sound of a roll up door being raised.

The scene shifts to an individual storage bay almost full of large plastic bags.

After a moment, Jake and Jenny enter.

                    JAKE
          This is it. Just as I left it.

                    JENNY
          And there are shoes in all those bags?

                    JAKE
          You better believe it. Here, let me show
          you.

He reaches for the nearest bag and pulls it open.

He reaches in and he removes a shoe box.

                    JAKE (CONT'D)
          See, this is heavy duty plastic. And
          each pair of shoes is in its original box
          packed for shipping.

He opens the box, parts the tissue wrapping paper and removes a high fashion very high-heeled shoe.

                    JAKE (CONT'D)
          This was a very popular number, sold like
          hot cakes.

He handles it fondly for a moment and hands it to Jenny.

                    JENNY
          Wow, what a beauty. And look at that
          heel. To tell the truth, even when I was
          young I was a klutz in a heel like that.
          How did Ginger Rogers dance so gracefully
          in shoes like these, I can't imagine.

                    JAKE
          Don't worry, there's a large variety of
          styles. You'll find some with
          comfortable heels. I hope you'll keep
          some for yourself, souvenirs from me.

                    JENNY
          Thank you.

Suddenly, Jake seizes her and kisses her on the lips.
She is stiff for a moment, acquiesces briefly, and then
pushes him away.

                    JENNY (CONT'D)
          Please, Jake, not so fast.

                    JAKE
          I'm sorry, Jenny, I'm really sorry.

                    JENNY
          Don't apologize, it's not necessary.
          Just be patient.

                    JAKE
          Patient? For a young person, maybe
          patience is a virtue. At my age, it's
          lunacy.
                    (a beat)
          Please forgive me.

                    JENNY
          It's okay.

She spots a crate and sits down on it.

                    JENNY (CONT'D)
          You're a good kisser.

He sits on a crate next to her.

                    JAKE
          Some compliment. Believe me, I'm out of
          practice.

                    JENNY
          Believe me, I'm out of practice, too.

                    JAKE
          We should practice together.

They chuckle. A pause.

                    JAKE (CONT'D)
          It wasn't supposed to happen like this.
          I gave a lot of thought to how to
          approach you. Like a teenager, I
          rehearsed in my mind even how I would
          first drape my arm around you. I planned
          on saying cute things to you, preparing
          you, amusing you, even distracting you.
          My one strategy was not to risk acting in
          a way that could possibly offend you.

                    JENNY
I looked over my horoscope earlier today.
There was a paragraph about romantic
opportunities, but I skipped over it. I
figured it was irrelevant.

                    JAKE
I hope I'm not irrelevant.

                    JENNY
Of course not, you and Jules are very
important to me.

                    JAKE
Jules? Oh, that fellow we see from time
to time at the retirement home.

                    JENNY
I glanced at your horoscope, too.
        (she laughs)
It said you should seize opportunities.

                    JAKE
I guess I did that. And don't tell me,
you looked at Jules' too?

                    JENNY
I did. It said he should resist the
tendency to hold back as he has a lot to
offer.

                    JAKE
I don't like that. Please don't tell him
and put ideas in his head. It will only
confuse him.

A pause.

                    JAKE (CONT'D)
Jenny, you know I care for you.

                    JENNY
Yes.

                    JAKE
I love you.

                    JENNY
I love you too.

                    JAKE
But, not just as a friend?

She smiles enigmatically. She rises and begins to poke
about the area. She pauses at a carton on the floor.

                    JENNY
          Oh, what's in here?

                    JAKE
          It's a record player.

                    JENNY
          Does it work?

                    JAKE
          Sure.

                    JENNY
          Do you have any records?

                    JAKE
          In the box next to it.

                    JENNY
          What type of music?

                    JAKE
          Popular music from the thirties, forties
          and fifties.

                    JENNY
          Wonderful. Let's take them with us.

                    JAKE
          Do you want to?

                    JENNY
          The corner of the recreation room would
          make a nice dance floor space. Do you
          like to dance?

                    JAKE
          Listen, I'm a taller...and slightly older
          version of Fred Astaire when he was in
          his prime. Let me select a few pairs of
          shoes for you before we leave.

                    JENNY
          Oh, thanks. Jake, I can arrange for the
          cancer agency to picks the shoes up here.
          Is that all right with you?

                    JAKE
          Sure, it saves me schlepping these bags
          around.

                        JENNY
              Good, it means a lot to me.

As the lights dim on the storage space, music is heard -
a slow, sentimental ballad. It continues for quite a
while and then the scene shifts to a space in the
recreation room. Jenny and Jake are dancing.

Jules, stone-faced, sits nearby watching. They dance
well with many dips and twirls. When the music ends Jake
and Jenny face each other. He bows, she curtsies.

Jake goes to the record player. He selects another
record.

                        JAKE
              Let's try this one.

He puts the record on, returns to Jenny. It's a swing
record.

                        JENNY
                    (dubious)
              You want to try this?

                        JAKE
              You bet.

They begin to dance, not crazy but fairly fast. They
know how. Suddenly, Jake stops, breathing heavy.

                        JENNY
              Are you okay?

                        JAKE
              Just out of breath.

                        JENNY
              Maybe you ought to sit down.

                        JAKE
              Maybe I ought to sit down.

Jake sits down. Concerned, Jenny studies him.

                        JAKE (CONT'D)
              I'm all right.

He shoos her away. She goes to the record player,
terminates the fast number, and substitutes another
record, a slow number.

She approaches Jules, arm outstretched.

Mr. Greenblatt, a man in his eighties and confined to a wheel chair, enters and positions his chair near Jules.

                    JENNY
          It's your turn.

                    JULES
          Well, no, I don't care to.

                    JENNY
          Oh, come on, don't be a party pooper.

                    JULES
          I don't dance.

                    JENNY
          You don't dance?

                    JULES
          I can't dance.

                    JENNY
          I'll teach you.

                    JULES
          I'm not teachable.

                    MR. GREENBLATT
          Listen, sweetheart, I'll dance with you.
          If I could stand up, I would dance with
          you.

Tenderly, Jenny strokes Mr. Greenblatt's face.

The music continues as the lights fade.

The following morning:

Jules is sitting on his customary bench reading his newspaper in the customary way. Jenny approaches. He becomes aware of a presence and lowers his paper. He is surprised to see Jenny.

                    JENNY
          Good morning, Jules.

                    JULES
               (joking)
          Oh, hi, I didn't recognize you here just
          standing still. Not running today?

                    JENNY
          I thought I'd skip it this morning.
               (she sits down on the bench)
                         (MORE)

                    JENNY (CONT'D)
I wanted to tell you Jake telephoned me
this morning from his room. He said he's
feeling a little tired and just wants to
stay in bed for awhile. He tried to
reach you in your room but you had
already left.

                    JULES
          (rises)
That doesn't sound right, I'll go check
on him.

                    JENNY
Wait.
          (Jules sits again)
His voice was strong and he insists he
just needs to rest. But, I notified the
head nurse anyway and they're sending a
nurse to his room. I think it's better
to let the professionals handle it.

                    JULES
Yes, I think that's best.

                    JENNY
Do you want to go back to reading your
paper?

                    JULES
No, no, please.

                    JENNY
I don't want to interrupt your routine.

                    JULES
          (self-mocking)
Routine it is, that word describes it.
I'm a man with deeply ingrained habits,
or routines.

                    JENNY
Is that bad?

                    JULES
Yes, it can be. My wife used to complain
I wasn't spontaneous. But then again she
wasn't so spontaneous herself.

                    JENNY
How long were you married?

                    JULES
Forty-five years.

                    JENNY
A long time.

                    JULES
A long time.

                    JENNY
You have one child, I understand.

                    JULES
Yes, a son. He's a bachelor. A
certified public accountant.

                    JENNY
Do you see him often?

                    JULES
No.

                    JENNY
He must be very busy.

                    JULES
It's not that, I'm sure.

                    JENNY
You're not close?

                    JULES
No. And I don't know why. I'm an
introspective fellow, I've searched for a
reason without success. Well, there's a
saying, a camel cannot see his own hump.
Maybe I'll have to content myself with
this being unexplained. He seemed happy
enough as a kid. I was there for him, we
had fun. I don't know, he acts like he
has a grievance.

                    JENNY
Why don't you ask him?

                    JULES
I could do that, I suppose. On the other
hand, maybe the answer is simply that
he's a jerk. It happens.

                    JENNY
If I were you I'd talk to him. But, then
again you didn't ask for my advice, did
you?

                    JULES
I think I did in my devious, indirect
manner.

                    JENNY
My approach to situations like that is to
try like hell to resolve them as opposed
to...well, not doing anything.
          (a beat)
Okay, that ends my advice column for
today. When I sat down here you didn't
think you were getting "Dear Jenny."

                    JULES
          (emotionally)
Dear Jenny is exactly the way I think of
you.
          (a pause)
It seems a little strange just sitting
here talking to you, alone. But I have
to admit, I like it.

                    JENNY
So do I.

A pause.

                    JULES
Do you know the average age of the
residents here?

                    JENNY
I've read their brochure, they say it's
eighty-five.

                    JULES
That's right. And that means Jake and I,
who are in our late seventies, are mere
youngsters around here. And further, it
means, that you are at such a tender age,
comparatively speaking, you could be
considered a mere child.

                    JENNY
A mere child, I like that.

                    JULES
I think there are members of the staff
who are older than you. I didn't think
anyone so young could become a resident
here.

                    JENNY
Yes, I think you're right. But I had
"pull", a cousin of mine is on the board
of directors here.

                    JULES
Oh.
          (half beat)
Which brings us to the next question...
Why would a younger, vital woman wish to
retire among such an old population?

                    JENNY
Yes, that's the question. Jules, I
wouldn't have minded if you had just
asked me directly.

                    JULES
I told you I'm a devious fellow, that
encompasses, "complicated."

                    JENNY
I don't think you're devious, I do think
you're complicated in the sense there are
some things you can't deal with directly.
Well sometimes, I can't either. I came
here because they have a skilled nursing
facility. I'll be needing it soon. I
have cancer, an aggressive form. It's in
remission now, and I'm feeling well, but
the doctors expect it to return. I just
have a small pension to live on, and no
immediate family. For me, this is the
best place to be under the circumstances.
In a way I'm glad you asked because I've
been debating with myself whether to tell
you and Jake, or just let matters take
their course.

                    JULES
          (stunned)
Oh, Jesus. Jesus Christ.

                    JENNY
Not that I mind, but his name is not
usually invoked around here.

Sobbing, he embrace her.

                    JENNY (CONT'D)
It's all right, Jules, it's all right.
Jules, it's all right.

The sound of an ambulance siren is heard nearby. It
grows very loud and suddenly stops.

                    JENNY (CONT'D)
               (alarmed)
          Jake? I hope it's not for him.

                    JULES
          Let's go.

Together, they hurry off.

END OF ACT I

ACT TWO

                    NARRATOR
          I hate to tell you this - that sometimes
          when we expect the worst, it's true,
          although most of the time, it's not. In
          this case, the ambulance was indeed for
          Jake. Now, a day later, Jules is at the
          hospital, waiting in what is
          appropriately called a waiting room.

A hospital waiting room. Jules is alone. He is sitting
down sipping coffee from a Styrofoam cup. On the table
next to him is another cup with the lid in place. He
glances at his watch, he is getting antsy.

After a while, Jenny enters.

                    JENNY
          I'm sorry I kept you waiting.

                    JULES
          What kept you?

He offers her the coffee on the table. She takes it and
sits down.

                    JENNY
          Thanks.

She removes the lid from the cup, sips.

                    JULES
          You seem agitated.

                    JENNY
          Something very interesting happened, I'm
          a little excited.

                    JULES
I'm all ears.

                    JENNY
Oh, first let me tell you. I spotted
Jake's doctor doing his notes at the
nurse's station and I spoke to him. He
said the procedure inserting the new
defibrillator went well. Jake is doing
fine and could be discharged as early as
tomorrow.

                    JULES
Great news. That guy really had me
worried.
          (a pause)
Shall we head back or do you want to tell
me about your "interesting" experience
now?

                    JENNY
          (she sits)
I went back to see Jake.

                    JULES
How come? We already said good-bye to
him.

                    JENNY
I just had this strong feeling I should
go see him again. I went into his room
which was pretty dark. He was lying in
bed flat on his back. I spoke to him
softly but he didn't answer. I went to
the side of his bed and looked down at
him. Clearly, he was awake. I thought
he was about to doze off or was in a
funny mood of some kind. I bent over the
bed to kiss him good-bye and suddenly he
grasped my hand and held it in a strong
grip. He spoke to me in a course
whisper. He said, Jenny, my mind is
clear, I'm not doped up or anything. I
want you to know that I love you and I
want to marry you. Jenny, will you marry
me?

                    JULES
Why that son of a gun!
          (half beat)
How did you handle it?

                    JENNY
Handle it? I said yes.

                    JULES
WHAT?!

                    JENNY
Is that all you can say?

                    JULES
What do you want me to say?

                    JENNY
How about "congratulations" or "mazeltov"
if you prefer.

                    JULES
Oh, come on, Jenny, you can't be serious.
He took advantage of you. That was a
shameless thing he did.

                    JENNY
I don't see it that way. But I am a
little shook up. I don't know what made
me go back into his room, but receiving a
marriage proposal, I assure you, was not
uppermost in my mind.

                    JULES
Of course not. Well, don't worry about
it...
          (he laughs)
He's not going to sue you for breach of
promise.

                    JENNY
He'll have no reason to.

                    JULES
I don't really believe this. You're just
toying with me, aren't you?

She shakes her head from side to side continuously.

                    JULES (CONT'D)
You really intend to go through with
this?

She shakes her head up and down continuously. Jules
scrutinizes her. A pause.

                    JULES (CONT'D)
          (curtly)
Let's go, we need to get a jump on the
evening traffic.

He rises abruptly and starts for the exit. She rises and
follows. The lights fade.

Music is heard - something familiar with a love and
marriage theme, done with a satirical edge. Lights dim.

Lights up on the following morning:

Jules is on his customary bench, reading his paper in his
customary manner with the paper held in front of his
face.

After a while he lowers the paper, looks down the walk
from which Jake usually approaches. He sees nothing and
raises his paper again.

After a while he lowers the paper again, looks down the
walk, sees nothing. He looks at his watch, then raises
his paper again. After a while, Jenny approaches walking
purposefully.

                    JENNY
          Jules, we need to talk now.

Jules lowers his paper.

                    JULES
          I don't do confrontations before
          breakfast.

                    JENNY
          Then let's call it a frank exchange.

                    JULES
          That's diplomat-eese for confrontation.

                    JENNY
          Don't hide behind your fancy language.
          In any case, I can use big words, too.

                    JULES
          Oh, yes, you're a college graduate, a
          librarian no less. Then you have the
          advantage, my dear, because I never went
          to college.

                    JENNY
               (sits)
          Stop this nonsense. I need to know
          what's bothering you.

                    JULES
          And I thought you just wanted to talk
          about your wedding plans.

                    JENNY
          Damn it, Jules, I want you to stop this.
          Something's bothering you, have the guts
          to say what it is. I don't need to
          surmise what it is, you need to say what
          it is.

                    JULES
          All right, why are you going along with
          this farce? By that I mean, as if you
          didn't know, Jake's proposal and your
          acceptance.

                    JENNY
          It's not a farce, a lovely man asked me
          to marry him and I accepted.

                    JULES
          Lovely man? The lovely man manipulated
          you with the oldest trick in the world,
          he appealed to your better nature, he
          played the sympathy card and you went for
          it hook, line, and sinker.

                    JENNY
          None of that matters. Jake loves me and
          I love him.

                    JULES
          Then this is really idiotic. The lovely
          man has had two heart surgeries and a
          recent incident. It's pathetic, how
          vulnerable he is. He's barely alive so
          what's this wedding stuff all about?
          It's a joke, a big joke, a colossal joke,
          nothing less. And while we're at it,
          what about you? Does he even know about
          your medical condition? For Christsake,
          the two of you are nothing more than
          walking corpses!

                    JENNY
          I feel sorry for you.

She rises and walks off. He is motionless for a time,
then he covers his face with his hands and begins to sob.

                    JULES
          And I love you both.

The lights dim.

                    NARRATOR
Well, there seems to be trouble in the
ranks of the three musketeers. But not
even Alexander Dumas could have predicted
that two of the musketeers would decide
to marry each other and the excluded
musketeer would react with a combination
of jealousy, remorse, impotence to alter
the situation, and above all, love for
the others. Complicated emotions. Perhaps
this is what comes of mixing the genders
in the ranks of the musketeers.

The following morning.

Jules' bench. Jules is seated staring straight ahead.
After quite a while he turns to his newspaper on the
bench and raises it in front of his face in his usual
manner.

In a while, Jake approaches.

                    JAKE
What's the news of the day?

                    JULES
          (hesitates)
Same old, same old.

He lowers the paper, looks at Jake. They are silent.

                    JAKE
So?

                    JULES
So?
          (a beat)
You look okay.

                    JAKE
Why not? For three days I had nothing to
do but sleep and rest in between naps.
Now, I feel great, refreshed, raring to
go.

                    JULES
Raring to go where?

                    JAKE
          (flamboyantly)
Up and down life's pathways, wherever
they take me.

                    JULES
Yes, very poetic.

                    JAKE
I'm such a remarkable person, I have many
talents.

                    JULES
Obviously.

A pause.

                    JAKE
All right, Jules, what's going on with
you?

                    JULES
Didn't Jenny tell you?

                    JAKE
She told me you're not so happy with the
idea of our getting married.

                    JULES
        (warily)
Did she tell you what I said?

                    JAKE
She told me you were very upset, and you
upset her. But you know, Jules, if she
hadn't said a word to me, I could tell
right away something's eating you. Where
was the, Hey, Jake you lucky dog!
Congratulations! I wish you all the
best! That's what I had a right to
expect, but what did I find sitting here?
Some bitter guy I don't even recognize.

                    JULES
Feel free to leave at any time.

                    JAKE
Right now I feel free to sit here and ask
you what this is all about.

                    JULES
Then to avoid disappointing you again,
I'll give it my best shot. It's about an
old guy with such an awful medical
history he has to walk on eggs just to
stay alive, suddenly getting all excited
about getting married. That's stupid.

                    JAKE
That's not stupid. What you just said is
stupid. Don't you think I understand I'm
at risk. So what? Sure I could drop
dead the next minute. You're a healthy
guy and you could, too. And that goes
for younger people, too. I didn't have
to wait for the wisdom of old age to
figure that out.

                    JULES
From where I sit I don't see any wisdom.
I see foolishness. And please try to
curb your excitement. One trip to a
hospital in an ambulance this week should
be enough.

                    JAKE
I'm not in a particular hurry to die, but
when it comes it comes. Right now I'm
alive so pardon me if I act like I'm
alive.

                    JULES
Calm down.
        (a beat)
Do you know about Jenny's condition?

                    JAKE
Yes.

                    JULES
So?

                    JAKE
We'll deal with it together.

                    JULES
        (sarcastic)
That's very loyal of you.

                    JAKE
Loyal, yes, and your sarcasm was not lost
on me. If I take an oath in sickness and
in health I mean in sickness and in
health. If sickness comes, I will be
there with her every minute. She will
not have to face it alone. She will know
she is loved and she is not alone.

                    JULES
        (again sarcastic)
Yes, you're an honorable man.

                         JAKE
          Exactly.

A long pause.

                         JAKE (CONT'D)
                    (softly)
          Let's go in for breakfast.

                         JULES
          I've made other plans.
                    (he reaches for his
                     newspaper)
          And please don't bother me anymore.

Jules returns to his paper. Jake rises and exits.

The lights fade.

Lights up on the rabbi's study.

The rabbi, an older man who speaks with an accent, is
seated at a table with Jake and Jenny. He is looking
down at a document.

                         RABBI
          All right, if you leave the marriage
          license with me I'll prepare the wedding
          certificate. So when do you want to get
          married?

                         JAKE
          Right away.

                         RABBI
          This minute?

                         JENNY
          In the next few days, if you can fit us
          in you schedule.

                         RABBI
          I can fit you in. Tomorrow at three.

Jake and Jenny exchange a look. They are happy.

                         JAKE & JENNY
          Yes.

                         RABBI
          You'll have a lot of guests?

                    JAKE
          Just the people who live here who want to
          come.

                    RABBI
          No family members?

Jenny shakes her head no.

                    JAKE
          I have two daughters. They can't come.

                    RABBI
          Why can't they come?

                    JAKE
          They live far away. And, I contacted
          them, they don't approve.

                    RABBI
          It's an old story, young people are
          embarrassed when their parents have young
          ideas. They think young ideas are their
          private property. Also, this makes sense
          at least, they worry about their
          inheritance.

                    JAKE
          It will be all right, they're good kids.

                    RABBI
          So, do you want a ceremony with all the
          bells and whistles or just the blue plate
          special?

                    JAKE
          Blue plate special?

                    RABBI
          By that I mean, I cut to the chase, no
          flimflam.

Jake and Jenny exchange a look and laugh.

                    JENNY
          Rabbi, we'll leave it to your good
          judgment.

                    RABBI
          That's probably a big mistake.
               (a beat)
          So, I think we have covered everything.
          Wait a minute, do you need any marriage
          counseling?

Jake and Jenny exchange a look and laugh.

                    JAKE
          No, Rabbi, thank you, but we don't need
          marriage counseling.

                    RABBI
          You don't, but I do. That's another
          story.

They start to exit

                    RABBI (CONT'D)
          Oh, why didn't you bring Jules? I'm not
          used to seeing you without him. He'll be
          the best man, of course.

                    JAKE
          I'm not sure. He's not speaking to us.

                    RABBI
          He should come anyway. Best man is not a
          speaking role.

They exit. Lights dim.

Klezmer music is heard, segues to more traditional
wedding music.

Lights up on section of the recreation room. Four men
are holding up each corner of the wedding canopy
(chuppa). Jake is waiting under the canopy, the rabbi is
waiting off to the side.

The wedding march is heard being banged out on a piano
and Jenny enters. She joins Jake under the canopy.

The rabbi comes closer, looks out front, standing before
the unseen congregation. He chants a prayer in Hebrew
and then sings.

                    RABBI (CONT'D)
          For those of you who do not know what we
          are going to do here, or who wandered in
          by mistake, this will be the wedding of
          Jake Rosenberg and Jenny Rosen. They met
          here at Golden Years Leisure Living.
          They have not known each other very long,
          so I guess this is what they call love at
          first sight. Last month I conducted the
          marriage of a couple in their nineties,
          and last year I conducted the weddings of
          three couples, all of them in their
          eighties.
                    (MORE)

                    RABBI (CONT'D)
You could say romance flourishes here at
The Golden Years Leisure Living. Maybe
it's something in the atmosphere, or
maybe the cook is putting something in
the food. But the best explanation, I
think, is the natural impulse of most
people to live two by two, to be a
couple, to have a partner in life. Why
not? It's not always so easy to find
your way in his labyrinth called life.
And this way, if you are lucky, you will
have a helping hand. Of course, at this
age, I don't have to remind the couples
of their obligation to be fruitful and
multiply. Their multiplying days are
over. On the other hand, the Almighty
did not bless the marriage of our
patriarch Abraham and his wife, Sarah,
with a child until they were over a
hundred years old. Anything is possible.
So maybe there were more miracles in
those days, or maybe the miracles are
still occurring, but they are more
subtle, or we are too busy to notice. In
any case, my fellow rabbi's - at the drop
of a yarmulke so to speak, can explain it
all to you. After all, it is part of
their job description to explain
everything, very clearly, even if it is
unexplainable. For myself, I can live
with the mystery of things. I think we
must all accept and live with the mystery
of things. Do we have a choice? Now I
must say an additional brief word about
the elderly who marry. I realize it is a
joke to some people and even kind people
indulge themselves in a little smile. To
those people I say, you should deepen you
understanding. The elderly are not
merely survivors, they are the veterans
who have seen much, endured much, and
often experienced great sorrow in their
lives. They are the heroes of human
existence.

The Rabbi turns to Jake and Jenny, positions them to face
each other. He speaks to them privately.

Jules enters and stands off to the side.

The rabbi reads from a book in Hebrew for a moment.

                    RABBI (CONT'D)
          Jake, the rings?

Jake takes the rings out of his pocket and hands them to the Rabbi. Rabbi hands one to Jake and one to Jenny.

                    RABBI (CONT'D)
          Please place the ring on Jenny's finger.

Jake does.

                    RABBI (CONT'D)
          Jenny, place the ring on Jake's finger.

Jenny does. The Rabbi joins the hands of Jake and Jenny.

                    RABBI (CONT'D)
          Do you, Jake Rosenberg take Jenny Rosen
          to be your wife?

                    JAKE
          I do.

                    RABBI
          Do you, Jenny Rosen, take Jake Rosenberg
          to be your husband?

                    JENNY
          I do.

                    RABBI
          I pronounce you husband and wife. Okay,
          that's it, you're married.

Jake and Jenny embrace and kiss. Jules abruptly turns and exits. Guests surround the beaming couple.

The lights fade.

Happy, bucolic music is heard.

Lights up on Jenny sitting on a bench reading a book. Jules approaches, somewhat tentatively.

                    JULES
          What are you reading?

                    JENNY
               (looks up)
          A book.

An awkward pause

                    JULES
          Can I talk to you?

She nods yes. He sits.

                    JULES (CONT'D)
How are you?

               JENNY
I'm fine.

               JULES
And Jake?

               JENNY
He's fine. He had to make an emergency
visit to the dentist this morning, yet
he's still fine.

               JULES
I'm glad.
        (a beat)
I want to wish you and Jake great
happiness.

               JENNY
Thank you. I'm sure Jake would like to
hear that too directly from you.

               JULES
        (nods)
Yes, I'll tell him.
        (a pause)
Please forgive me for what I said to you.
I think it's the ugliest thing I've said
to anyone in my life. I can't tell you
how ashamed I am.

               JENNY
All right, don't dwell on it.

An awkward pause. Jules rises.

               JULES
Well, that's what I wanted to say.

               JENNY
Oh, sit down, Jules.

He sits. A pause. Finally, she smiles

               JENNY (CONT'D)
You can get rid of that hang dog
expression and we can talk.

               JULES
        (tries to smile)
Okay.

                    JENNY
A hell of a musketeer you turned out to
be.

                    JULES
I guess I violated the code.

                    JENNY
Well, I guess you had to deal with a
unique situation. In any case, you get
another chance.
          (a beat)
There's something I'm curious about.

                    JULES
Okay.

                    JENNY
You asked me why I came to live here at a
comparatively young age, and I told you.

                    JULES
Yes.

                    JENNY
Well, you were seventy-five when you came
here. And for a very healthy, vigorous
man what was your hurry to enter an "old
age" home?

                    JULES
Ah, you think I made my move too early?

                    JENNY
The question is, what do you think?

                    JULES
I think your question goes to the heart
of the matter.

                    JENNY
This is like pulling teeth....and the
heart of the matter is?

                    JULES
Very simple, I was looking for a refuge.

                    JENNY
A refuge?

                    JULES
Yes, a refuge. As in here, I have a
room, and grounds, and a dining room.
                    (MORE)

                    JULES (CONT'D)
As in here, there is a skilled nursing
facility, if it proves necessary, and as
in here, there is still another facility
if I get Alzheimers or become totally
disabled. You see, this is my one stop
last stop refuge. My very last refuge.
I just wait here for the end, which is
more or less the way I've lived my entire
life...waiting for the end.

          JENNY
How sad.

          JULES
Yes, sad, and don't think I don't know
it.

          JENNY
But why?

          JULES
You don't want me to make a fool of
myself again, this time as I try to
diagnose my problem.

          JENNY
I want to hear whatever you care to tell
me.

          JULES
I lived the way I lived because I
couldn't do otherwise. I couldn't help
myself.

          JENNY
Did you seek professional help?

          JULES
No.

          JENNY
Why not?

          JULES
I couldn't.

          JENNY
So you were trapped in a trap partly of
your own making?

          JULES
Yes.
          (a beat)
          (MORE)

                    JULES (CONT'D)
I have to say, I can't look back on my
life with satisfaction. In fact, it is
with self-loathing.

                    JENNY
               (alarmed)
There were good things, I'm sure.

                    JULES
I enjoyed reading. You're a librarian, a
literary person, let me share a literary
moment with you. Once, when reading from
James Boswell's Journals, I came across
this entry, which I have memorized -
"Friday, 11 February, 1763. Nothing
worth putting in my journal occurred this
day. It passed away imperceptibly, like
the whole life of many a human
existence." When I read that it was like
a dagger thrust into my heart. It
described so perfectly my life.

                    JENNY
You may be getting a little too operatic
about this. You had a life, a marriage,
a child, a career.

                    JULES
I had to do something while I was waiting
to die.

                    JENNY
Tell me about your career in the "CIA."

                    JULES
               (laughs)
Well, I did really work for a government
agency, a local agency, the Department
of Sanitation to be specific. For a long
time, I was the guy who dispatched the
refuse trucks. After many years I began
to work my way up the ladder of success.
Finally, I did achieve a prestigious
position as an administrator with a lot
of responsibility and a very satisfactory
living.

                    JENNY
Okay, and why didn't you go to college?
Obviously, you're a very intelligent man.

                    JULES
Stupidity. Who said you can't be
intelligent and stupid at the same time?

                    JENNY
          Yeah, we see a lot of examples of that,
          don't we?

They fall silent. A long pause.

                    JENNY (CONT'D)
          I love you, Jules.

                    JULES
               (touched)
          Oh? Does that mean if I'd asked you to
          marry me first, you would have accepted?

                    JENNY
          Probably.

                    JULES
          If you don't mind my saying so, you're a
          pretty strange woman.

                    JENNY
               (cheerfully)
          I know.

                    JULES
          I love you too.

                    JENNY
          I know.

Slowly, they begin to laugh. Jake approaches. Jules gets
up.

                    JAKE
          I didn't expect this from you, I didn't
          deserve this from you. You were my best
          friend, the best friend I ever had. You
          sonofabitch, how could you do this to me?

Jake begins to push Jules, very hard, his palms thrusting
against his shoulders and driving him back.

                    JAKE (CONT'D)
          You sonofabitch, you sonofabitch!

                    JENNY
          (SHOUTING) Jake! Stop! Jake, stop this!
          Stop! Jake!

Jake stops, seems uncertain. Suddenly, he embraces Jules
in a bear hug.

> JAKE
> You sonofabitch, I love you. I love you.

They are embracing.

Smiling, Jenny looks on.

The lights fade.

Note: During the narration that follows the following montage takes place:

Jenny at a word processor, typing speedily, confidently.

Jake removing a shoe box from s stack of shoe boxes. He opens it, removes a shoe, admires it, and then with the shoe in hand and the box in the other, he exits presumably about to fit a customer.

Jules sitting at a desk engaging in a phone conversation. His shirt collar is open, his necktie askew. He snaps up another phone on his desk and now is engaged in two phone conversations.

Back to Jenny still typing as before. Suddenly. She stops a look of pain and fear on her face. One hand slides down to her abdomen and she holds it there for quite a while. Finally, she returns to her typing in a very measured and deliberate manner. She is working through her pain.

> NARRATOR
> There was a need for more volunteers at
> the cancer agency that Jenny was involved
> with. The agency had recently opened new
> stores and acquired an additional truck.
> Jake readily agreed to join with Jenny in
> volunteering, but Jules resisted.
> However, Jenny insisted and Jules
> surrendered. They did good work. Jake
> with his charm and years of experience in
> the retail business was a big help in the
> stores. Jenny was invaluable in staffing
> the stores, doing office work, soliciting
> contributions. She did it all. But oddly
> enough, the super star of the volunteers
> was Jules. There was a management gap at
> the Agency, and Jules with administrative
> and supervisory experience was the ideal
> person to fill the gap. They got
> involved, their juices were flowing. They
> worked hard, they loved it. After six
> weeks of this, Jenny began to experience
> a return of her symptoms.
> (MORE)

                    NARRATOR (CONT'D)
They were mild, not yet disabling, but
Jenny recognized what was happening. She
made an appointment to see her doctor but
she was not yet ready to tell Jake or
Jules what she was experiencing. On their
day off, and the day before her scheduled
visit to her doctor, she told the men she
would like to re-visit the Pacific
Palisades in Santa Monica. They agreed.

Lights up on the same bench overlooking the ocean.

Laughter and the voices of Jules, Jake and Jenny are
heard off stage.

It is a lovely morning. They approach the bench.

                    JENNY
               (excited)
This is it, the same bench as last time.

                    JAKE
Of course, I reserved it.

                    JULES
               (wiping an area with his
                handkerchief)
You forgot to inform the birds.

They sit, Jenny in the middle.

                    JENNY
               (looking out)
It's such a lovely day.

                    JAKE
Great.

                    JULES
Wonderful.

Jenny looks down and to the side.

                    JENNY
Oh, where's our little friend? I was
looking forward to seeing him again.

                    JAKE
He'll be here. I guarantee it.

                    JENNY
I hope so, but what makes you so sure?

                    JAKE
          Trust me. And just in case he needs a
          little encouragement...

Jake removes a bag of peanuts from his pocket and
scatters some near the bench.

                    JULES
          You brought peanuts, well, so did I.

Jules removes a bag of peanuts from his pocket and
scatters some near the bench.

                    JENNY
          My heroes.

                    JAKE
          Come on out, you little rascal.

                    JENNY
          Look, there it is!

                    JAKE
          See, it went right for one of my peanuts.

                    JULES
                 (to Jake)
          Sorry, old fellow, that was one of my
          peanuts.

                    JENNY
          Now, now, boys, let's not have a contest
          about your peanuts.

They laugh. They fall silent. They look out.

                    JENNY (CONT'D)
          I'm so happy.

A long pause

                    JENNY (CONT'D)
          I've just had such an interesting
          thought. I was thinking of Madama
          Butterfly who lived all the way across
          this ocean. I thought of her betrayal by
          Lt. Pinkerton and her tragic death. And
          then I contrasted her life with mine.
          Here I am, safe, secure, loved, so happy
          in the company of the men I love. You may
          think it's too much of a stretch to
          compare opera and a real life, but I
          think now there is no important
          difference.
                    (MORE)

>   JENNY (CONT'D)
>   Sometimes, we may smile at what seems the
>   excessive passion in the opera. But,
>   they are right, we must have passion in
>   our lives.

Beat.

>   JENNY (CONT'D)
>   Yes, passion.

She turns to Jules, strokes his cheek.

>   JENNY (CONT'D)
>   You need more.

She turns to Jake. Strokes his cheek and then kisses his
cheek.

>   JENNY (CONT'D)
>   You have enough.

They are looking out at the ocean. Jenny takes their
hands.

Music from Madama Butterfly is heard.

The lights slowly fade.

END OF PLAY

UNCLE DAVID WINS THE LOTTERY

EVE, 60

DAVID, 65

YOUNGER EVE, 40

YOUNGER DAVID, 45

STEVE, 25

JANE, 25

EUGENE, 35

The year is 1999.

The dining room of a Spanish type house built in the
Fairfax district of Los Angeles in the 1930's. The rooms
are spacious and bright with high ceilings. EVE, 60,
enters from an interior room. She speaks directly to the
audience.

> EVE (TO AUDIENCE)
> I am going to tell you the story of
> David. David Kipnis, a very boring man. I
> say boring not to insult him, not to
> deprecate him, just to be factual. This
> man ventured nothing in his life,
> experienced very little and since he is
> not exactly an intellectual heavyweight
> ... Well... What is there? The fact that
> he is grumpy, opinionated and repetitious
> completes the picture. David lives here
> but don't jump to conclusions. He is not
> my husband or my lover or... so, what is
> he doing here? Good question. But it's a
> long story so I'll save it for later.
> Maybe he could be described as my roomer,
> my boarder and now... my roommate. No, I
> don't like the sound of that at all.

DAVID, 65, enters from his bedroom. He appears
bedraggled, ill. He walks with an almost imperceptible
limp yet he uses a cane. He approaches Eve. She is
shocked by the expression on his face.

                    EVE (CONT'D)
You look terrible. You haven't been
looking at all well lately. Are you sick?

          DAVID
Something happened.

          EVE
What happened?

          DAVID
Something happened.

          EVE
Alright, David, I will stipulate that
something happened. The question is...
what happened?

          DAVID
You won't believe this.

          EVE
Well, tell me.

          DAVID
You won't believe this.

          EVE
Here we go again. David, maybe I will
believe it, and maybe I won't. Just tell
me what happened.

          DAVID
It's incredible.

          EVE
David!

          DAVID
First, promise you will keep what I tell
you a secret.

          EVE
No.

          DAVID
Why not? Is that so much to ask?

          EVE
Yes, it is.

          DAVID
Why are you being so unreasonable?

                    EVE
If you consider it unreasonable, so be
it.

                    DAVID
I don't understand your hostility. All
I'm asking is that you keep a confidence.

                    EVE
No. We've known each other too many
years, if you don't trust my judgment, my
intelligence, my ability to act
appropriately, well... too bad.

                    DAVID
All I asked was that you not tell
anybody.

                    EVE
I am not in the mood to make any
promises, so don't share your secret with
me.

She turns her back to him and starts to exit.

                    DAVID
I won the California Lottery.

She stops in her tracks, turns to him.

                    EVE
You what?

                    DAVID
Yes, I won the California Lottery.

                    EVE
That's impossible.

                    DAVID
I would agree with you. Except that it
happened.

                    EVE
But you hate the lottery. For years I had
to listen to you complain about the evil
lottery, the stupid people who play and
your boast that you never bought and
never would, buy a lottery ticket in your
entire life.

                    DAVID
That's true.

                    EVE
          So explain.

                    DAVID
               (Shrugs)
          I bought a ticket, I won.

                    EVE
          That's no explanation.

                    DAVID
          I will tell you, but don't you want to
          know how much I won?

                    EVE
          Yes, David, how much did you win?

                    DAVID
          Eighty-four million dollars. But after
          they take out the taxes and the discount
          for the cash payment, I'll be lucky if I
          clear fifty million.

                    EVE
          Poor fellow.

A long pause. Eve rises.

                    EVE (CONT'D)
          I don't appreciate your joke.

She begins to exit.

                    DAVID
          It's not a joke!

Eve sits down - opposite David.

                    EVE
          Really, what is this all about?

                    DAVID
          You heard somebody won the big prize last
          month, didn't you?

                    EVE
          Yes.

                    DAVID
          And if you listen to the news, you also
          know that the winner has not yet claimed
          his prize.

                    EVE
Yes.

                    DAVID
That's me. I am the winner!

                    EVE
And you haven't claimed the prize?

                    DAVID
That's right.

                    EVE
So what are you waiting for?

                    DAVID
        (Dolefully)
I'm waiting.

                    EVE
David, tell me what happened.

                    DAVID
I was in the supermarket. I passed the
lottery vending machine. For some reason
I went back to it and put in a dollar.
Then I didn't know what to do. I stopped
a man who was walking by - a black man
but he was very nice, and asked for help.
He said do you want to play the super
lotto. I said yes and he touched the
screen. He said do you want cash value.
That sounded alright so I said yes. So he
touched the screen. He said do you want
the quick pick? I said, "what is that?"
He said that was when the computer makes
the selection for you. I said, "we live
in a computer age, so let the computer
choose." He touched the screen and then I
heard a funny noise from the computer and
I saw my ticket come out of the machine.

                    EVE
I see. And where is the ticket now?

                    DAVID
Here in my wallet.

David taps the outside of his hip pocket.

                    DAVID (CONT'D)
Naturally, I keep it with me.

                    EVE
Naturally. David, you checked the numbers
carefully? Your eyesight isn't so
wonderful and these tickets are printed
very lightly. I should know.

                    DAVID
I used my magnifying glass and I double
checked and triple checked and quadruple
checked and quintuplet checked...

                    EVE
Quintuplet?

                    DAVID
It was a joke...I think.

                    EVE
I'm glad you located your sense of humor.

                    DAVID
        (Panicked)
I am terrified!

                    EVE
        (Shouting)
What is your problem? You just won a
great fortune, you are now rich and
powerful. Maybe a little jubilation is in
order!

                    DAVID
Jubilation? Rich and powerful? I am still
the same man I was before I won the
lottery.

                    EVE
        (Studies him)
I see what you mean. But you might
discover that suddenly becoming a multimillionaire has some impact on who you
are.

                    DAVID
But I don't want an impact, I want no
impact, I want to be left alone. The idea
of all that attention, the notoriety,
just the thought of it scares me to
death. I need to live a quiet life, to
follow my pattern, my routine, that's
what I want.

                    EVE
Most people would put up with a little
inconvenience to be a multimillionaire.

                    DAVID
I am not most people!

                    EVE
Yes, David, I need no convincing.

                    DAVID
I don't know what to do.

                    EVE
If ever there was problem with a simple
solution this is it.

                    DAVID
What? What? Tell me.

                    EVE
Give the ticket away.

                    DAVID
Are you crazy?

                    EVE
I'm just trying to be helpful.

                    DAVID
So let me guess who I should give the
ticket to.

                    EVE
You don't have to guess, give it to me.

                    DAVID
To you? After what you did to me? You are
crazy! That will never happen! Never!

                    EVE
              (Incredulous)
What did I do to you?

                    DAVID
You know!

                    EVE
I don't know! I haven't a clue!

                    DAVID
You know!

                    EVE
GODDAMNIT, David, I don't know what the
hell you're talking about!

                    DAVID
Liar!

                    EVE
I don't know what you're talking about!!!

                    DAVID
You know!

                    EVE
I don't know!

                    DAVID
You raised my rent.

                    EVE
I raised your rent?

                    DAVID
Aha! Now you have the effrontery to deny
it.

                    EVE
          (Realizing)
But that was twelve years ago. I raised
your rent twenty dollars a month. The
only time in all the years you've lived
here.

                    DAVID
So you admit it. You knew I lived on a
very tight budget but you raised my rent.
You are a greedy landlord and you should
be ashamed of what you did.

                    EVE
For your information, I live on a very
tight budget too. And to this very day
your rent is probably twenty-five percent
of the going rate. What the hell do you
want?

                    DAVID
Don't change the subject. You raised my
rent, it is not something that I will
forgive or forget. Never!

> EVE
> I don't believe this. And you have been
> carrying around all this anger and
> resentment all these years. Well, make it
> easy on yourself and do me a big favor at
> the same time - get out of my house! I
> want you out! As of this minute you are
> evicted. Out! Out!

David is somewhat intimidated but he manages to hold his
ground.

> DAVID
> No. I have legal rights.

> EVE
> What legal rights? You have no legal
> rights.

> DAVID
> Of course, I do. Everybody has legal
> rights. I'll get a lawyer and I'll sue.

> EVE
> Don't make me laugh.

> DAVID
> Notice. I'm entitled to notice before you
> evict me.

> EVE
> Alright, I give you notice. Thirty days
> as of this minute. Now get out of my
> sight.

Forgetting his cane, David starts to withdraw. At the
doorway he turns to her.

> DAVID
> You bloodsucker landlord!

He exits. Eve picks up his cane and hurls it in his wake.
She is very anxious. She paces the room, uncertain what
to do. After a moment she goes to a cabinet and removes a
bottle of whisky. She pours herself a shot and downs it.
She pours another one. She sits in a straight backed
chair against the wall and speaks directly to the
audience.

> EVE (TO AUDIENCE)
> Did I tell you that David could be very
> irritating? And did you imagine that a
> woman like me might have a slight
> drinking problem?

She gets another drink and returns to the same chair. The
lights dim on Eve as the sound of a door opening and
closing are heard from the street entrance. YOUNGER EVE,
40, and YOUNGER DAVID, 45, using his can for an
imperceptible limp, enter. They wear dark clothing. The
mood is somber. YOUNGER EVE sits listlessly on the sofa,
YOUNGER DAVID sits opposite her.

                    YOUNGER DAVID
          Can I get you something? A glass of
          water?

                    YOUNGER EVE
                (Distracted)
          Oh, no thanks.

                    YOUNGER DAVID
          If you need anything, anything at all...

                    YOUNGER EVE
          I'm alright.

                    YOUNGER DAVID
          Maybe I shouldn't mention it now, but
          some people were a little disapproving
          that you had him... the cremation.

                    YOUNGER EVE
          It was what Harry wanted and I don't care
          if people disapprove.

                    YOUNGER DAVID
          There was also some grumbling because
          people weren't invited here after the
          memorial service for a bite to eat.

                    YOUNGER EVE
          Too bad.

                    YOUNGER DAVID
          But the most serious complaint is your
          decision not to sit shiva.

                    YOUNGER EVE
          David, I really don't give a shit what...

                    YOUNGER DAVID
          What I want to say is I agree with all
          your decisions.

                    YOUNGER EVE
          Yes, thank you.

                    YOUNGER DAVID
Are you sure I can't get you something? A
glass of water, tea, instant coffee? I
make the best instant coffee.

                    YOUNGER EVE
               (Tries to smile)
I'm okay, David.

                    YOUNGER DAVID
I'm sure you're very tired.

                    YOUNGER EVE
Yeah.

                    YOUNGER DAVID
There's something we need to talk about
as soon as possible. Obviously, this is
not a good time. Maybe a little later
when you're rested.

                    YOUNGER EVE
If it's so important, you can tell me
now.

                    YOUNGER DAVID
No, no, it can wait.

                    YOUNGER EVE
David, it's okay, tell me.

                    YOUNGER DAVID
I want to tell you that I will make
arrangements to move as soon as possible.
I realize this is a delicate situation.

                    YOUNGER EVE
What delicate situation? And what's this
about moving?

                    YOUNGER DAVID
Well, listen, Eve, I understand. I am not
such a fool.

                    YOUNGER EVE
Quit beating around the bush. If you have
something to say, say it.

                    YOUNGER DAVID
Well, you know our status now. You are a
widow, still young and I am a bachelor,
still not so old. Not such an ideal
situation. People talk.

                    YOUNGER EVE
Ah, yes, the propriety of the situation.
But aren't you forgetting Stevie lives
here too?

                    YOUNGER DAVID
Stevie is five years old. Not exactly the
correct age for a chaperone.

                    YOUNGER EVE
Chaperone? Forgive me if I am amused by
the use of that term. David, if you are
in any way uncomfortable about remaining
here, by all means, move, at your
convenience. I don't think it's necessary
but suit yourself.

                    YOUNGER DAVID
You don't want to think about it?

Younger Eve shakes her head "No." David is relieved.

                    YOUNGER DAVID (CONT'D)
Maybe I can be helpful. I could watch
Stevie when you go to the store. Things
like that.

                    YOUNGER EVE
Yes. Things like that.

                    YOUNGER DAVID
I am happy we had the opportunity to
discuss this. To be truthful this is like
my home and I prefer to remain. Well, you
must be worn out and I am a little
exhausted myself.

He exits to his room. Younger Eve watches Younger David
exit. She lingers for a moment and then exits to her
room.

The lights go up on Eve still sitting in the straight
backed chair against the wall.

                    EVE (TO THE AUDIENCE)
As you can see, David was a pillar of
strength in my hour of need. I really did
want him to stay. After all, he was a man
and I was used to having a man around. I
was alone and afraid.

After a few moments, she rises and exits to her bedroom.
Almost immediately we hear the sound of voices at the
front door entrance.

STEVE, 25, JANE, African-American woman, also 25 enter.
They are kissing until Jane pushes Steve away.

>   JANE
>   Hey, come on. Your mom's car is in the
>   driveway. We shouldn't do this when she's
>   home.

>   STEVE
>   Why? She knows I'm crazy about you.
>   Besides, she's probably taking a "nap"
>   now.

Steve removes a liquor bottle from the cabinet and
inspects the level of booze left.

>   STEVE (CONT'D)
>   Yep, I'd say she's "napping" soundly.

>   JANE
>   That's not nice.

He puts the bottle down and turns to Jane.

>   STEVE
>   Hey, I have something important to tell
>   you.

>   JANE
>   What?

>   STEVE
>   I'm horny as hell right now. I need you
>   this minute! (laying it on thick) Your
>   great beauty arouses a passion in me that
>   knows no bounds. Let us retire
>   immediately to our boudoir.

>   JANE
>   You sound like the last of the great
>   romantics. And no wonder you're the last.

>   STEVE
>   Do not judge me too harshly. I am crazed
>   with passion.

He takes her hand and starts to pull her along. She
breaks away.

>   JANE
>   No, she'll wake up. She'll hear us.

>   STEVE
>   Don't you think she hears us at night?

                    JANE
          It's different during the day.

                    STEVE
          Yeah, it's more fun.

She breaks away from him decisively. He sits in a chair,
buries his face in his hands and feigns sobbing. She
stands beside him and strokes his hair.

                    JANE
          It's alright, baby just be patient.
          Tonight... we love.

David enters from his room.

                    DAVID
          Am I interrupting something?

                    STEVE
          No, no, we're just clowning around.

                    DAVID
          Clowning around. As if you had any other
          activity.

                    STEVE
               (to Jane)
          Well, I think I'll rest up for tonight's
          activities.

Steve exits to his bedroom.

                    DAVID
          Maybe he should try resting at night for
          daytime activities, like *work*. I think
          you are a smart girl so you probably have
          already figured out he's a bum.

                    JANE
          He's trying to get a handle on things.
          Maybe he needs to hear more encouragement
          and less carping.

                    DAVID
          I think it may be too late for anything
          except to throw him out in the street.
          But that of course would deprive *you* of a
          home too.

                    JANE
          You'd like that, wouldn't you?

                         DAVID
                    (Heartfelt)
          You are mistaken. You don't understand,
          that boy is breaking his mother's heart.
          And...

                         JANE
          ...And yours too.

David does not reply.

                         JANE (CONT'D)
          I'll make tea.

David nods almost imperceptibly. She enters the kitchen
area behind the counter and pours water into a teapot and
places it on the stove. David sits forlornly at the
dining room table. After a moment, Eve enters, hesitates
when she sees David and appears ready to go back to her
room when Jane becomes aware of her.

                         JANE (CONT'D)
          We're having tea. Join us?

Eve decides to sit at the dining room table. David does
not stir. They are silent. Anger, embarrassment,
contrition hang in the area. Jane, serving the tea, is
aware of their strange mood. She joins them at the table.
A long awkward silence ensues.

                         EVE
                    (To Jane)
          So, did David tell you the good news?

                         JANE
          Good news? You could have fooled me.

                         EVE
          Yes, good news. Good news, isn't it,
          David?

                         DAVID
                    (Flatly)
          Yes, good news.

                         JANE
          I'd hate to be here if something tragic
          happened.

A long pause.

                         JANE (CONT'D)
          Well, I'd certainly like to hear the good
          news.

                    EVE
David won the lottery.

                    JANE
          (Skeptical)
Oh, sure. Well, that certainly is good
news. I once won a fifty dollar raffle.

                    EVE
David won eighty four million. Isn't that
right, David?

                    DAVID
Yes. Eighty four million. But that's
before taxes.

                    JANE
Please don't inform the IRS but I didn't
report my winnings.

                    EVE
But, Jane, we're not joking. Are we,
David?

                    DAVID
          (Depressed)
We're not joking.

                    JANE
I'm not joking either. Well, gee, David,
what do you plan to do with all that
money?

                    DAVID
I haven't decided to take the money.

                    JANE
But why not?

                    DAVID
I don't want it, I don't need it.

                    JANE
But think of all the people you could
help. You could make a lot of people very
happy.

                    DAVID
People should make themselves happy. They
shouldn't bother me about their
happiness.

                    JANE
        But isn't that part of your tradition?
        Charity, helping the unfortunate members
        of society.

                    DAVID
        If by my tradition you mean the Jewish
        religion, I can assure you I am not a
        dues paying member.

                    JANE
        I see.

Steve enters.

                    STEVE
        You guys having a party?

                    JANE
        Yeah.

                    STEVE
        I could tell by the festive mood.

                    JANE
        Well, it's a tea party.

                    STEVE
        That it explains it.

Steve sits. Jane rises to get him a cup of tea, then
joins them. Steve surveys the scene.

                    STEVE (CONT'D)
        So what's new and exciting?

                    JANE
        Funny you should ask.

                    STEVE
        Oh...

                    JANE
        Your Uncle David won the lottery.

                    STEVE
                (Playing along)
        yeah, that's new and exciting.

Slowly, methodically, David removes his wallet and
extracts a lottery ticket. He also removes a much folded
newspaper clipping. He lays them on the table closest to
Steve. Steve picks up the lottery ticket.

> STEVE (CONT'D)
> Looks like a lottery ticket.

Steve takes out the newspaper clipping.

> STEVE (CONT'D)
> And this looks like a newspaper clipping
> with the winning lottery numbers.

Steve falls silent as he scrutinizes the paper before
him.

> STEVE (CONT'D)
> ... I need paper and a pencil!

He leaves the table precipitously and runs into the
kitchen and returns immediately with a pad and pencil. He
hands them to Jane.

> STEVE (CONT'D)
> Write down these numbers.

Steve reads from the lottery ticket.

> STEVE (CONT'D)
> Seven, thirty one, twenty four, two, ten,
> thirty. Got them? Now read them back.

> JANE
> Seven, thirty one, twenty four, two, ten,
> thirty.

> STEVE
> Now cross out the numbers when I read
> them. Two, twenty four, seven, thirty
> one, seven, ten.

> JANE
> All the numbers are crossed out!

> STEVE
> Then this is the winning ticket! *This is
> a fucking winning fucking ticket! Uncle
> David! You've won the fucking lottery!
> You're rich, rich, rich, rich, rich,
> rich!*

He rushes to David, kisses him on the cheek. David
cringes and deftly takes the ticket from his hand,
otherwise does not react. Steve kisses his mother, who
remains seated stoically. He pulls Jane from her chair to
dance with her and they try, without success, to get
David and Eve to leave their chairs and form a circle.

David folds the lottery ticket and calmly replaces it in his wallet. He rises and walks toward the exit to his room. There he turns and wags his finger wildly at the others.

> DAVID
> Not even one penny for any of you!

He exits.

> STEVE
> What was that all about?

> EVE
> Didn't you know, I am a bloodsucker landlord which makes you the son of a bloodsucker landlord and that makes you (points to Jane) the girlfriend of the son of a bloodsucker landlord.

She rises and exits to her room.

> JANE
> You know, you white people are very strange.

BLACKOUT

The lights come up on the living room. It is late afternoon. Eve enters from the area ordinarily used by David to enter and exit. She appears worried.

> EVE (TO THE AUDIENCE)
> It's five o'clock and David isn't home yet. So what's the big deal? For David it must be a big deal because he is a man of rigidly fixed habits. He hates to deviate from his schedule. If he does, the world, *his* world anyway, is severely out of joint. At five on weekdays David is always found waiting in front of his TV waiting for the news with Wolf Blitzer to come. Currently, Wolf Blitzer is the newscaster David most admires. He says having to grow up dealing with a name like "Wolf" probably helped develop his character. Come to think of it, what were the Blitzers thinking when they named their son Wolf?

She goes to her liquor cabinet, removes a bottle and pours a drink. This time, as she continues speaking, she nurses her drink in a very controlled manner.

                    EVE (CONT'D)
David and my husband, Harry, worked as
cutters in the same clothing factory.
When Harry and I bought this house we had
to scrape together every dime we had and
commit ourselves to a monthly payment
that seemed near impossible. So it seemed
like a good idea for David, a bachelor,
to come live here. The men enjoyed each
other's company and the extra money
helped. And David did not make waves.

She looks outside to see if David is in sight. No luck.

                    EVE (CONT'D)
Well, it couldn't be car trouble that is
delaying him because David never owned a
car. Or anything of value, for that
matter. David, in fact, had nothing. No
wife, no children, no job, no friends, no
hobbies - just us. And we had him. About
a year after he came to live here David
was hit by a truck while he was crossing
the street. He sustained a broken hip
among other injuries. He recovered and he
also recovered what must have been a
fairly substantial settlement. How much,
he never said. We know he bought
government bonds with the money and ever
since he has lived off the interest. As
you can tell from his lifestyle, he does
not need a lot of money to pay his
expense. So, when he was in his forties
he was already a completely retired
gentleman. Maybe that explains in part
why he was not so excited about winning
the lottery. If the goal of winning is
not to have to work anymore he had
already achieved that. So in a sense, he
had already won the lottery.

David enters from the front door. He looks worn out. He
sinks into the sofa.

                    EVE (CONT'D)
You're late.

                    DAVID
So, Wolf Blitzer will have to go on
without me tonight.

Silence. His breathing is heavy.

                    DAVID (CONT'D)
          I've got a lot on my mind, a lot of
          issues to deal with.

                    EVE
          I see.

                    DAVID
          I telephoned the lottery office,
          anonymously. I asked the question if
          someone wins the big prize and wishes to
          remain anonymous, is that possible. I was
          told *no* because the public must see there
          is a real-life-and-blood winner, or they
          will not trust the lottery.

                    EVE
          That seems reasonable.

                    DAVID
          They are liars. They want the excitement,
          the publicity, the hullabaloo to attract
          more suckers to buy tickets.

                    EVE
          As one of the suckers you did ok with
          your dollar investment.

A pause.

                    DAVID
          I have been very nervous lately. I know
          sometimes I say and do stupid things when
          I am that way. I hope you can overlook
          it.

                    EVE
          Forget it.

He rises.

                    DAVID
          Maybe I'll go watch Greta Van Susteren.

                    EVE
          Oh, do you like her?

                    DAVID
          She is shrill and excitable. She invites
          people on her program and then with her
          interruptions she won't let them talk.
          But it's a pleasure to see a homely woman
          on TV for a change.

He exits to his room. Eve sits, reflects, smiles at her
recollections.

> EVE (TO THE AUDIENCE)
> There were other occasions, minor
> incidents, when David surprised me by
> deviating from his rigid pattern, but
> then there were a few times when the shoe
> was on the other foot. And no doubt the
> situation was far more important.

The lights dim on Eve. The lights rise on the remainder
of the room as Younger David turns away from looking out
the window and begins to pace the room. It is very late
at night. He is wearing a robe and slippers. His hair is
in disarray and it is clear that he is very agitated. He
continues to pace, veers to the window again to look out.
He goes to the telephone, stares at it trying to decide
if he should make a call. At one point, he actually picks
up the phone about to dial. He replaces the phone. The
sounds of a key being inserted and of a door opening are
heard and Younger Eve enters. She has had a drink or two
but she is not inebriated, more exhausted than anything.
He turns on her fiercely.

> YOUNGER DAVID
> Where have you been?!

> YOUNGER EVE
> What?

> YOUNGER DAVID
> Do you realize what time it is?!

> YOUNGER EVE
> It's four A.M.. It's three minutes after
> four A.M. To be exact. I stand corrected.

Younger Eve sinks into the sofa.

> YOUNGER DAVID
> What, you think this is a joke? You think
> this is funny? Don't you know how serious
> this is? Do you have any idea how worried
> I was?

> YOUNGER EVE
> I had no idea how worried you were, but
> I'm beginning to get the idea. I'm sorry,
> David, that you worried.

                    YOUNGER DAVID
I was crazy, I didn't know what to do! I
was going to call the police. I had the
phone in my hand to call the police.

                    YOUNGER EVE
The police? Why would you call the
police?

                    YOUNGER DAVID
To report a missing person! To report a
possible crime. To report an accident. To
have them search the hospitals.

                    YOUNGER EVE
Again, I'm sorry that you reacted this
way, but you're getting a little carried
away, don't you think?

                    YOUNGER DAVID
You have no consideration for me! When
you are out late I can't fall asleep
until I hear you come home.

                    YOUNGER EVE
You're not my parent.

                    YOUNGER DAVID
I am not your parent, I would not want to
be your parent!

                    YOUNGER EVE
And I wouldn't have you for a parent!

                    YOUNGER DAVID
You know I am a light sleeper! How could
you torture me like this?

Younger Eve gets up.

                    YOUNGER EVE
Alright, David. You've had a chance to
ventilate. I am really sorry you were
alarmed. We're both exhausted so let's go
to bed.

                    YOUNGER DAVID
No, no, no, no. I want to know what kind
of woman you are. Where is your self
respect to stay out until the middle of
the night?

Younger Eve is livid but in control. She sits down
slowly, speaks with deliberation.

                    YOUNGER EVE
David, I don't have to account to you for
my conduct but in this instance I choose
to do so. This week Stevie is away at
camp and I am taking vacation time. So
this was a window of opportunity for me,
so to speak. I went out by myself in
search of a good time and as it turned
out, I had a good time. Do you want me to
be more specific?

                    YOUNGER DAVID
Why didn't you tell me you would be out
late? All you had to do was tell me you
would be late.

                    YOUNGER EVE
David, I acted spontaneously. The word
spontaneous is, I'm sure, in your
vocabulary, but I doubt it's in your
lexicon.

                    YOUNGER DAVID
Do you think this fancy talk will conceal
your bad behavior? You should be ashamed.

                    YOUNGER EVE
It's time to wind this up so I'll be
blunt. Tonight I went to a bar. I met a
man, and I went to his apartment and we
fucked. In case you haven't noticed,
David, I am a mature woman.

                    YOUNGER DAVID
A mature woman does act that
way...sometimes.

The lights dim in this area and go up on Eve sitting in
the straight backed chair against the wall.

                    EVE (TO AUDIENCE)
Oh, David. David, David, David, David...

BLACKOUT

The lights come up on the living room. Day. Steve is
sprawled on the sofa going over the classified pages of a
newspaper. He has a pen in one hand. Jane is seated
nearby studying a thin paperback version of a published
play.

                    JANE
See anything interesting?

                    STEVE
          Yeah, two or three that I'll probably
          check out.

                    JANE
          Probably?

                    STEVE
          Well, yeah, sure, I'm gonna follow up.

                    JANE
          Is that the Sunday paper?

                    STEVE
          Yeah, the Sunday paper has the most job
          ads.

                    JANE
          But today's Tuesday.

                    STEVE
          I know. What's the big deal?

                    JANE
          The big deal is you should have looked at
          the ads on Sunday so you could start job
          hunting first thing Monday morning.

                    STEVE
          Aw...c'mon...

                    JANE
          Clearly, you're going about this in a
          half assed way.

                    STEVE
          Clearly, you're beginning to piss me off.

A strained silence. Suddenly Steve plunges his fist
through the newspaper, crumples it and throws it on the
floor.

                    STEVE (CONT'D)
          This is bullshit! My Uncle David is a
          multi-millionaire and here I am looking
          in the paper for some crappy job.

                    JANE
          So now he's "my Uncle David."

                    STEVE
          I've always called him Uncle David.

                    JANE
          Yeah but in a mocking kind of way.

                    STEVE
          That's only been lately.

                    JANE
          That's not what I heard.

                    STEVE
          You don't know anything.

                    JANE
          I know it's been years since you two were
          civil to each other. You told me.

                    STEVE
          I got pretty crazy in my teens, he didn't
          like it. But we've always been close,
          like family. Hell, we *are* family.

                    JANE
          He knows you're an addict. The last thing
          you can expect from him is that he'll put
          money in your hands.

                    STEVE
          I'll convince him. And I'll go back to
          college and get my degree. I can do it.
          You believe me, don't you?

                    JANE
          Less and less.

                    STEVE
          Jane, please don't give up on me.

                    JANE
          I'm trying not to.

                    STEVE
          It will work out with Uncle David, I know
          it will. Look, I'm all he's got, me and
          my mother and maybe you...he really likes
          you.

                    JANE
          I like him.

David, using his key, admits himself from the front door.
He enters the living room.

                    STEVE
          Oh, hi, Uncle David. Having a good day?

David grunts his disapproval.

                    DAVID
          You don't have to worry about my day.

Jane shoots Steve a look that says, "you fool."

                    STEVE
          Well, I've got to get ready for those job
          interviews I was telling you about.

Steve exits to his room.

                    DAVID
          If I wait here for him to come out
          dressed for a job interview, I will wait
          a very long time.

                    JANE
          Please try to be patient with him.

                    DAVID
          Sometimes we run out of time before we
          run out of patience.

He sits quietly alone with his thoughts. As she observes
his sadness. It's almost palpable.

                    JANE
          Are you all right?

He replies with an inconclusive gesture.

                    JANE (CONT'D)
          I think I'll make tea.

He just sits there. She goes to the kitchen, puts the
kettle on.

                    JANE (CONT'D)
          It'll only be a minute. Would you rather
          have it at the dining room table or in
          the living room?

                    DAVID
          All right.

                    JANE
          I'll take that to mean it doesn't matter.

He picks up the script she was reading, studies it with
interest.

                    DAVID
Chekhov...

                    JANE
What...

                    DAVID
Chekhov, you are reading Chekhov.

                    JANE
Oh, I'm going to do a scene from Uncle
Vanya for my acting class.

                    DAVID
So you want to be an actress? I know that
already, but do you *really* want to be an
actress?

                    JANE
Yep.

                    DAVID
I think many young people are attracted
to this profession. I can understand why.
But it is also my understanding that only
a relatively few succeed.

                    JANE
It's a tough business. The competition is
unbelievable.

                    DAVID
So why do you risk disappointment?
Heartbreak even?

                    JANE
I love it.

                    DAVID
You love it?

                    JANE
I do. I really do.

                    DAVID
I think that is the best reason to do
something.

He is still holding the play. He looks down at it
contemplatively. Jane observes him.

                    JANE
Have you ever seen a Chekhov play?

                    DAVID
          Once, many years ago, it was on
          television.

                    JANE
          Did you enjoy it?

                    DAVID
          It was incredible.

                    JANE
          Which one?

He holds up the script he has in his hands.

                    DAVID
          Uncle Vanya.

They smile.

The tea kettle goes off and Jane gets the tea. She places
the tray on the coffee table and sits on the sofa beside
David.

                    JANE
          But did you never see one of his plays in
          a theatre?

                    DAVID
          I have read many of his plays. Three
          times a week I walk to the branch library
          - every Monday, Wednesday and Friday,
          from two o'clock to four o'clock. I read
          current events, history, some fiction,
          even a poem or two, and I read plays. I
          read Chekhov but I had to stop.

                    JANE
          Had to stop? Why?

                    DAVID
          I could not bare it any longer.

                    JANE
          What do you mean?

                    DAVID
          This writer has portrayed the loneliness
          and the despair of human beings like no
          one else. He has penetrated to the
          desolation of the human soul. For me it
          became too difficult to be involved.

                    JANE
Involved? You're a very sensitive man.

                    DAVID
I do not wish to experience pain, even
when it belongs to someone else.

                    JANE
But these were fictional characters.

                    DAVID
But that is the genius of you creative
people, you can make fictional characters
more real, more memorable than real
people.

                    JANE
What's your favorite play in all the
world?

                    DAVID
The Death of a Salesman by Arthur Miller.
It is, in fact, the only play I have seen
in a theatre in all my life.

                    JANE
You're kidding.

                    DAVID
Why should I kid about this?

                    JANE
I don't know but it almost seems that
way.

                    DAVID
So what is your question, Why is it my
favorite play or why is it the only play
I have seen in a theatre?

                    JANE
Well, yes, both.

                    DAVID
Why I never went again to the theatre?
Because the play is a masterpiece and I
did not think I could do better...

                    JANE
But that doesn't...

                    DAVID
...As for the play... here the writer has
penetrated the psyche of the American
people and what he wrote then is just as
true today. He wrote about the
exploitation of the worker by the
capitalist, he wrote about the tragic
consequences of holding foolish false
values and he wrote of love and
disappointment and betrayal in the
family.

                    JANE
What about Miller's contemporary,
Tennessee Williams? Many people think he
was better than Arthur Miller.

                    DAVID
I have read his plays and I admire him
greatly. But he was a Southern writer. A
Southern writer is a Southern writer.
They are not to be confused with regular
people.

                    JANE
Well, I'll never make that mistake again.

A pause

                    DAVID
I would like to confide a secret to you.

                    JANE
Yes?

                    DAVID
I, too, am writing a play. I have been
working on it for many years. The working
title of my play is The Death of a
Tailor.

                    JANE
Really, how interesting.

                    DAVID
I was once a tailor myself, a real
tailor, before I went to work in a
clothing factory.

                    JANE
That's great. I'd love to read it when
it's finished or, better yet, see it
produced some day.

                    DAVID
What chance is there, even if I find the
energy to complete it? And even if it is
a masterpiece who would produce it? It
takes a fortune to produce a play.

                    JANE
Is money really a problem for you?

                    DAVID
Money is always a problem.

                    JANE
For you? You could produce your play
yourself, you could build a new theatre,
for heaven's sake!

                    DAVID
Oh, the lottery.

                    JANE
Can I ask you a question? If you feel
it's none of my business, just tell me.
Do you still keep the lottery ticket in
your wallet?

                    DAVID
Of course, in my wallet.

                    JANE
Don't you think that's terribly risky?
You could be robbed. You could lose your
wallet.

                    DAVID
I am not the kind of man who loses his
wallet.

                    JANE
It could happen and that really is a
frightening prospect.

                    DAVID
Maybe I could lose my head over a
beautiful young woman with a beautiful
soul, but lose my wallet... never.

                    JANE
Why do you want to write a play?

                    DAVID
Maybe I can create something that will
endure. Willie Loman died more than fifty
years ago, yet he still lives.
                    (MORE)

                    DAVID (CONT'D)
          Hamlet was killed in the play four
          hundred years ago, yet he still lives. He
          cannot be killed, he is indestructible.
          And I can make the same observation about
          ancient plays.

He falls silent.

                    DAVID (CONT'D)
          I enjoyed our conversation very much.

He takes a final sip of tea.

                    DAVID (CONT'D)
          You make the best tea.

David rises and starts to exit. Before leaving the room
he turns suddenly and raise his arms flamboyantly.

                    DAVID (CONT'D)
          Attention must be paid!

He exits. Jane remains seated for a moment and then rises
and begins to return the tray to the kitchen. Steve
enters.

                    STEVE
          You two had a long conversation.

                    JANE
          Actually it was just a few minutes.

                    STEVE
          What did you talk about?

                    JANE
          Theatre mostly.

                    STEVE
          Oh, theatre. So you didn't talk about ...
          you know what.

                    JANE
          Just in passing. Nothing new.

                    STEVE
          Dammit. He really is a nutcase. Jane,
          listen, help me out. I really need a
          little loan.

                    JANE
          No.

                    STEVE
You sure gave that a lot of thought.

                    JANE
It's past the thinking stage and you know
it. The answer is and remains no.

                    STEVE
Hey, c'mon, don't be such a hard-ass. You
can manage a few bucks. Look, you get to
live here with free room and board, don't
I get credit for that?

                    JANE
You suck, you really suck!

                    STEVE
It's true, isn't it?

                    JANE
I live here to be with the guy I love.

                    STEVE
All I was saying is that with your part
time job waitressing and... well, you
have some spare cash, right?

                    JANE
Yes, it's right, I do have some spare
cash and yes, it's right, this living
arrangement is very convenient for me,
and yes it's right without you, it
wouldn't be possible, that is certainly
right!

                    STEVE
Okay, okay, don't bite my balls off.

                    JANE
And I want you to know that I understand
who my real benefactor is and it's not
you, it's your mother. And I also
understand it can't be easy for her, a
woman of her generation, to allow her
son's girlfriend to live in her house
with him and share his bed.

                    STEVE
Aw, that's no big deal.

                    JANE
Just maybe it is. God forbid you should
ever look at something from another
person's point of view.

                         STEVE
          Aw, she doesn't care. Besides, you're
          always helping out, every time I look
          around you're cleaning the house,
          scrubbing something.

                         JANE
          I try to be helpful, not that she's ever
          asked me, or implied that I should, I do
          it with love and with sense of gratitude.
          Yes, *gratitude, a fucking word that most
          certainly is not in your fucking
          vocabulary!*

Jane exits abruptly to their bedroom. Steve stands there,
uncertain, then exits from the front door. David,
agitated, enters from his room, looks about. Eve enters
from her room.

                         DAVID
          I heard yelling. I don't like yelling!

                         EVE
          *As your bloodsucking landlord, I take
          note of your complaint!*

Eve exits to her bedroom. David exits to his bedroom. In
a moment, Eve returns and goes to her liquor cabinet. She
removes a bottle and pours a drink.

                         EVE (TO AUDIENCE) (CONT'D)
          So what was that all about? He had
          already apologized, in his fashion, for
          the bloodsucker business and I had
          accepted, in my fashion, his apology. But
          these matters, personal hurts, are not so
          easily disposed of, are they? They fester
          and fester. I would like to tell you a
          little about David's background. His
          parents, German Jews, left Germany and
          came to the United States soon after
          Hitler came to power. So far so good. But
          they did not transplant well. They
          struggled economically and culturally in
          this foreign place, and when the war
          began and when the story of the
          concentration camps began to unfold and
          when they finally learned their entire
          family had perished in the holocaust,
          they descended into despair. For David,
          their only child, it must have been hell.
          (a Beat) Actually David was born here,
          but he still has... to my ears anyway, a
          slight foreign accent.
                         (MORE)

                    EVE (TO AUDIENCE) (CONT'D)
Well, that's David. Relations between
Stevie and David became complicated early
on. Stevie does not remember his father
but as for David... David was always
there. When Stevie was a little boy,
David played with him and read to him and
took him for walks holding his hand and
bought him ice cream. Which for David was
a major act of generosity. I think this
was the happiest time in David's life,
clearly he loved Stevie very much. Still,
as a father figure David was severely
impaired. There was no rough-housing, no
interest in sports, cars, mechanics,
fishing, whatever it takes to further the
bond with a developing boy. He didn't
even have an occupation that would give a
boy bragging rights. And, as it turned
out, Stevie became a difficult child
constantly causing problems at home and
at school. David, feeling frustrated and
impotent to change anything, withdrew as
an active presence in Stevie's life. And
that was fine with Stevie who wanted
nothing to do with the now sour old man
who lived in his house. But one thing is
certain, when people live under the same
roof there is bound to be some
interaction.

The lights fade on Eve. Younger David enters from his
room. He is agitated.

                    YOUNGER DAVID
     Eve... Eve!....

Younger Eve enters.

                    YOUNGER EVE
     David, what's all the excitement about?

                    YOUNGER DAVID
     I have something serious to tell you.

                    YOUNGER EVE
     What is it?

                    YOUNGER DAVID
     I don't like having to tell you this.

                    YOUNGER EVE
     Let me speed this up a little, it
     concerns Stevie, doesn't it?

                    YOUNGER DAVID
Yes.

                    YOUNGER EVE
Is he all right?

Younger David nods yes.

                    YOUNGER EVE (CONT'D)
Well, what happened?

                    YOUNGER DAVID
This is very serious.

                    YOUNGER EVE
David, I'm gonna throttle you.

                    YOUNGER DAVID
I found him in my room. He had my wallet
in his hand and he was removing a bill.

                    YOUNGER EVE
Oh, shit...

                    YOUNGER DAVID
I came into my room and I found him there
with my wallet in his hand. I said, *what
are you doing?* He said, *I didn't do
anything.* I said, *you are stealing my
money.* He said, *I didn't take anything.* I
said, *you are holding my wallet in your
hand.* He said, *I didn't touch your
wallet.* I said, *you are holding my money
in your hand.* He said, *I didn't touch
your money.* I said, *you are still holding
my wallet right in front of my eyes.* He
said, *I didn't do anything, I didn't do
anything,* and he dropped my wallet on the
floor and he ran out of the room. Eve,
this is very serious.

                    YOUNGER EVE
Yes, it is. As soon as he comes in I'll
talk to him and he'll be severely
punished.

                    YOUNGER DAVID
But this is serious!

                    YOUNGER EVE
Will you stop that? I told you I regard
this as serious.
                    (MORE)

> YOUNGER EVE (CONT'D)
> But it's not the end of the world, David,
> and he's not the first child to take
> money from a parent (she quickly corrects
> the word) from... someone.

> YOUNGER DAVID
> You don't understand. It's bad enough he
> was caught in the act stealing, but it is
> the *denial* that is so serious. The
> denial. If he won't even admit to
> something when he is caught in the act,
> if he refuses to take responsibility,
> then how can you expect him to change?
> Mark my words, Eve, it's the denial!

He exits in a huff. After a moment, Younger Eve exits to
her room. Lights up on Eve.

> EVE (TO AUDIENCE)
> It's the denial. Well David was right
> about that. And what was I saying about
> people under the same roof not being able
> to avoid interaction... or maybe even
> "attempted" interaction?

The lights go down on Eve and rise on Younger David and
Younger Eve. It is New Year's eve and music is heard form
the TV, a program leading up to the midnight celebration.
Younger David is sitting on the sofa. Younger Eve,
wearing an attractive frock, is standing nearby.

> YOUNGER EVE
> You promised. This year you'll stay up
> 'till midnight. And don't conk out on me.

> YOUNGER DAVID
> I'll do my best.

> YOUNGER EVE
> I have a bottle of sparkling wine in the
> refrigerator. We'll welcome in the new
> year together.

His eyes follow the picture on the TV screen.

> YOUNGER DAVID
> Such a hullabaloo. They're getting wild.

> YOUNGER EVE
> That's called celebrating. People do that
> sort of thing, you know.

> YOUNGER DAVID
> It's for young people.

                          YOUNGER EVE
          Not so long ago you told me that I was
          still young and you were not yet old.

He dismisses that comment with a gesture.

                          YOUNGER DAVID
          Tomorrow morning they'll wish they had
          more sleep and less to drink.

Dance music now heard. Younger Eve starts to move with
the music.

                          YOUNGER EVE
          Come on, let's dance.

                          YOUNGER DAVID
          You know I can't dance.

                          YOUNGER EVE
          I'll teach you.

She takes his hand. He resists but she forcefully pulls
him until, reluctantly, he rises.

                          YOUNGER DAVID
          Eve, I can't dance.

                          YOUNGER EVE
          Everyone can dance. You listen to the
          music and you just move your body. Come
          on.

Younger Eve pulls off her shoes as she holds onto Younger
David for balance. She tosses her shoes out of the way.
Younger David is awkward and not fully cooperating so she
helps position his hand on her back.

                          YOUNGER EVE (CONT'D)
          I'll lead, all you have to do is follow
          me. Get a little closer, I don't bite.

They dance. He is still awkward. He steps on her foot and
she breaks away.

                          YOUNGER EVE (CONT'D)
          Ow....

                          YOUNGER DAVID
          I'm sorry, I told you I can't dance.

She hops around for a minute and then returns to the
dance position. He is very reluctant.

                    YOUNGER DAVID (CONT'D)
          It's no good. I told you I can't dance.

                    YOUNGER EVE
          I'm alright. Tell you what, you take your
          shoes off too.

He does not welcome this idea but she is not about to
wait for a response. She places her palms on his chest
and pushes. He falls back on the sofa in a sitting
position. She raised one of his legs and pulls off his
shoe. She repeats this with his other leg. He looks down
at his feet.

                    YOUNGER DAVID
          I am happy I don't have a hole in my
          socks.

She extends her hand and helps pull him to a standing
position. They dance. This time it goes surprisingly
well. It's really looking good. Suddenly, he stops.

                    YOUNGER EVE
          What?

                    YOUNGER DAVID
          Suddenly, I have a headache, a migraine,
          I think. I need to take something strong
          and lie down.

He starts to exit, returns for this shoes and exits.

                    YOUNGER EVE
          Happy new year... coward... asshole.

Lights up on Eve.

                    EVE
          Asshole.

Mature Eve retrieves her shoes and exits to the bedroom.
Eve watches her exit.

                    EVE (TO AUDIENCE) (CONT'D)
          If I saw some potenital...of some kind,
          in David I also saw the futility of it
          all. Regarding my social, romantic,
          sexual, whatever you want to call it
          life, after Harry died it never really
          came together. There were occasional one-
          nighters, a few half ass relationships
          and maybe a couple that showed some
          promise, but eventually failed.
                              (MORE)

EVE (TO AUDIENCE) (CONT'D)
At those times, when one of my gentleman
callers was due to come to the house to
pick me up, I would subtly alert David,
who I knew had a little problem dealing
with the idea of my dating. And he would
make himself scarce. Economically, I
managed pretty well. I am a college grad
and I worked my way thorough college as a
bookkeeper. This is when the book keeper
was the nerve center of a small business
in a time before personal computers. For
small businesses I have a marketable
skill as a consultant, although I avoid
that term in order not to psyche them
out. On my business card I offer
accounting, advanced office services.
Advanced? That gets their attention. I am
self employed. I just work on a part time
basis. Stevie. Stevie is the immediate
problem. And the past problem. And the
foreseeable future problem. I agonized
about permitting him to live here, but I
didn't see a better choice. As to
allowing his girl friend to live here
with him, I'm not that comfortable with
it. But I'm trying to be hip. I even use
the "F" word on selected occasions. The
important thing, I think she maybe able
to help him. And the fact that she's
black, I'm not so comfortable with that
either. But I'm a life long liberal,
truly appalled by our nation's ugly
racial history, and maybe I'm trying to
prove something to myself, too. Well, the
bottom line is she's a mensch.

As for my drinking problem, it's slight. Very slight,
ever so slight.

She finishes her drink and exits.

BLACKOUT

The middle of the night, Jane, in her robe, is sitting
alone barely visible in the darkened room. After a while,
Stevie enters from the hallway near David's room. He is
just wearing his boxer shorts.

STEVE
Hey... Jane?

He switches on a table lamp.

                    STEVE (CONT'D)
What are you doing up?

                    JANE
That's what I want to ask you.

                    STEVE
Nothing... I couldn't sleep.

                    JANE
Why were you in David's room?

                    STEVE
I wasn't. I didn't go in.

                    JANE
I saw you come out of his room.

                    STEVE
No, I didn't go in, actually.

                    JANE
Tell me what you did.

                    STEVE
I didn't do anything.

                    JANE
You're after his lottery ticket, aren't
you?

                    STEVE
Are you crazy?

                    JANE
Yes. That's the only explanation for why
I stay with you.

                    STEVE
How can you accuse me of something like
that?

                    JANE
It's all too easy.

                    STEVE
I swear to God I didn't take anything.
Look, search me, go ahead and search me.

                    JANE
Don't act cute.

                         STEVE
No really. Think about it. If I took his
lottery ticket he'd blow the whistle on
me. My mom would blow the whistle on me.
You'd blow the whistle on me. I couldn't
get away with it. I'm not stupid.

                         JANE
So what were you doing in his room?

                         STEVE
I didn't go in. I just opened the door.
The way he was thrashing around in the
bed and crying out, it scared the hell
out of me. I think there's something
really wrong with him. I mean it.

                         JANE
Do you think it's a medical emergency?

                         STEVE
I think he was having one helluva
nightmare.

                         JANE
All right. So why did you open the door
to his bedroom?

                         STEVE
          (Desperate)
I don't know. I don't know what I was
doing.

A long pause.

                         JANE
Remember my friend Margaret? She's the
social worker I told you about. She told
me they have an outpatient hospital
program at Fairview for addicts, for
people with mental health issues. She
thinks it would be right for you.

                         STEVE
Who the hell is she? Mental health
issues! Maybe she ought to enroll in the
Goddamn program herself!

                         JANE
You need professional help.

> STEVE
> I just need to go back to college. You know I'm starting again beginning next semester.

> JANE
> In the meantime start the hospital program. You need professional help now.

> STEVE
> Look, even if I wanted to, where would I get the money? That can't be cheap.

> JANE
> You'll get the money. And if you don't, Margaret is a social worker, she'll know how to qualify you.

> STEVE
> I'll think about it.

> JANE
> No! I've been down that path with you before. I will not remain in a hopeless relationship, that's where I'm coming from.

She starts to exit, he goes with her.

> STEVE
> Jane, let's sleep on it to...

She stops abruptly, shoves him hard.

> JANE
> *You* sleep on the Goddamn sofa.

She exits. He withdraws to the sofa, sits, covers his face with his hands and begins to sob.

BLACKOUT

Day. Eve enters.

> EVE (TO AUDIENCE)
> Jane told me what happened. The next morning we agreed to check out the hospital program in more detail and if it was suitable, I agreed to pay unless it was more than I could possibly afford. In the past, Stevie had flirted with AA meetings an Narcotics Anonymous meetings but had refused to enter in any treatment program.
> (MORE)

                    EVE (TO AUDIENCE) (CONT'D)
So what he would do now was still up in
the air. Stevie was quiet, sullen,
depressed and staying out of our way. And
then something happened, and that, so to
speak, sucked up all the oxygen. What
happened? David went to the lottery
people with his winning ticket and turned
himself in as the culprit who had won the
lottery. As you can imagine, everything
else was put on hold. And surprise,
surprise, surprise, David appeared to
have *enjoyed* the entire experience. As
did we.

David, Jane and Stevie enter laughing. Eve joins them.
They sit around the coffee table.

                    STEVE
Uncle David, you looked great on TV. You
really looked great!

                    JANE
David, you have quite a presence, the
camera loves you.

                    DAVID
The camera loves me? So maybe I should
start a career on television. I could be
a newscaster. Dan Rather, look out!

                    EVE
I though you preferred Wolf Blitzer.

                    DAVID
I don't want to take away his job.

They laugh.

                    JANE
You were very poised and humorous. Do you
remember what you said?

                    DAVID
Do I remember? I was there.

Jane takes the remote control from the coffee table and
talks into it. She interviews David.

                    JANE
David Kipnis, who has been a resident of
the Fairfax district in Los Angeles for
many years, is the lucky winner of the
giant super lotto. David, how does it
feel to be the big winner?

                    DAVID
First, since I am old enough to be your
father, maybe even your grandfather, if
you address me as Mr. Kipnis I will be
happy to answer your question.

                    JANE
Oh, sorry. Mr. Kipnis, how does it feel
to be the big winner?

                    DAVID
I have no complaints.

                    JANE
Mr. Kipnis, many people, I'm sure, are
wondering why you waited so long to come
forth and identify yourself as the
winner.

She holds the remote control near his face.

                    DAVID
So what was the hurry? After all, Rome
was not built in a day.

                    JANE
Oh, yes, I see, you have a point there.
And now for the big, big question, What
do you plan to do with all that money?

She returns the remote control to his face.

                    DAVID
What do I plan to do with the money? Let
me answer your question by telling you a
Jack Benny story. Jack Benny was accosted
by a mugger who held a gun on him and
said, "Your money or your life." Jack
Benny didn't answer. The mugger became
impatient, "Which is it? Your money or
your life?" he demanded to know. Jack
Benny finally said... "I'm thinking it
over." And that is my answer to your
question - I'm thinking it over. I am
certain there are many people out there
who have suggestions and good ideas as to
how I should spend the money. And some,
no doubt, will attempt to contact me. So
I wish to say in advance that I decline
their help. I will take my time and
decide by myself what to do. Now, can I
take a moment to deliver a short
editorial?

                        JANE
          Editorial? Oh, well, yes.

                        DAVID
          I wish to speak to those who are
          titillated by the idea of winning the
          lottery. If you indulge your titillation
          by spending one dollar to buy a ticket to
          participate in this collective fantasy,
          well all right. But if you spend more in
          the hope of increasing your chance to
          win, you are mistaken. You are trying to
          apply logic to something that defies
          logic, and you are showing that you do
          not understand the law of random events,
          which is that there is no law governing
          random events. So do not allow the
          lottery people to entice you to throw
          your money away, and if the lottery and
          the state of California does not like
          what I am telling you... too bad. I am a
          man who speaks his mind, and this is
          America, it is a free country!

The others applaud.

                        STEVE
          Hey, Uncle David, the lottery is gonna
          put out a contract on you.

They laugh. The phone rings and continues to ring.

                        DAVID
          If it's for me, tell them I left for
          Mars.

The phone continues to ring. Steve answers.

                        STEVE
          Hello. What? (To David) The guy says he's
          Eugene Kipnis. He says he's your son.

                        DAVID
          What craziness is this?

                        STEVE
              (into phone)
          What craziness is this? Yeah... yeah...
          okay. (To David) He says he has absolute
          proof that he is your son. His mother's
          name was... hold on a sec (into phone)
          what's the name again? (To David) Wanda
          Willanski.

                    DAVID
          I never knew such a person.

                    EVE
          Of course you did, David. She worked in
          the shop with you and Harry. She was that
          mean Polish woman that nobody could
          stand.

David looks concerned.

                    STEVE
                (Into phone)
          Why don't you give me your phone number
          and I'll have him... Oh. (To David) He
          said he's right outside the front door.

Shocked, everyone is staring at the front door, frozen
expression on their faces.

BLACKOUT

ACT II

The action is continuous from the end of Act 1. Steve
puts down the phone and goes to the front door. He admits
EUGENE KIPNIS, about 35, wearing an expensive suit and
carrying an expensive brief case.

                    EUGENE
          I am Eugene Kipnis.

                    STEVE
          You better come in.

Eugene takes in the room in a glance. He walks directly
to David.

                    EUGENE
          Hello, father.

                    DAVID
          You're not going to kiss me, are you?

Eugene extends his hand for a handshake.

                    EUGENE
          How do you do, father?

                    DAVID
          How do you do?

They shake hands.

                    EVE
          You two should have some privacy for this
          ... Reunion?

                    DAVID
          Stay, stay!

Eve sits. Steve and Jane relax in their chairs. Eugene
opens his briefcase and removes a document.

                    EUGENE
          This is a certified copy of my birth
          certificate.

He hands the document to David who accepts it, gives it a
cursory glance.

                    EUGENE (CONT'D)
          You will note you are listed as the
          father, you will further note that the
          date of birth is consistent with the time
          of procreation. You may keep the document
          for your records.

                    DAVID
          You're a lawyer?

                    EUGENE
          No, I am not.

                    DAVID
          You sound like a lawyer. Eve, doesn't he
          remind you of a lawyer?

Eve shrugs.

                    EUGENE
          I know you have many questions. If you'll
          allow me to proceed in a narrative
          fashion I'm sure I'll anticipate and
          answer most of your questions.

                    DAVID
          He sounds so much like a lawyer.

                    EUGENE
          I regret to inform you that my mother
          Wanda Wallansky died a few years ago.
          Before she died she told me for the first
          time about you. She said she wanted a
          child but she did not want a husband.
                    (MORE)

                    EUGENE (CONT'D)
She said she chose you, in spite of the
fact that you were somewhat strange,
because she felt you had special
qualities, but she did not elaborate on
what they were. She said another reason
she chose you was because you were
Jewish. She said it was her belief that
Jewish men were a lot smarter than
gentile man.

                    EVE
If you would like to know of the
exception to prove the rule...

With a glance, Eugene reproves her interruption.

                    EUGENE
My mother also told me of her decision
never to inform you of her pregnancy. And
if you think back, you will be able to
reconstruct that shortly after the time
of conception she disappeared.

                    EVE
That's true. I mean nobody knew what
happened to Wanda. She disappeared
suddenly without a trace. But wait a
minute, if you knew about David when your
mother died, why did you wait so long to
contact him? The timing is very
interesting.

                    EUGENE
I'm coming to that! I, as you will soon
understand, am a very busy man. In my
line of work, information is king. One
gathers information in advance so that it
is available when, and if, it is needed.
That explains how I know all about you,
father, where you live and how you live.
I even know your bank balance, and as we
both know you were virtually out of funds
when you won the lottery. As for you,
Mrs. Gold. I know the essentials of your
life story and how you live today. And I
know about you unfortunate son, and his
long standing problem with drugs. And I
know about you, Jane Cousins and your
ambition to be an actress. You are not
strangers to me and the mystery is that I
am still a stranger to you now that you
have learned my name.
                    (MORE)

> EUGENE (CONT'D)
> I am Eugene Kipnis, venture capitalist
> and one of the richest men in America.
> And if that doesn't ring a bell with you,
> maybe this will help.

Eugene removes some magazines and newspaper clippings
from his briefcase and distributes them as he speaks.

> EUGENE (CONT'D)
> Here is a copy of *Time Magazine* when I
> made the cover. This is *Newsweek* when I
> was on their cover. These are clippings
> from *The Wall Street Journal* when they
> did a profile of me and in this issue of
> *Fortune Magazine* they wrote about me.

> DAVID
> What about *U.S. News* and *World Report?*
> They didn't put you on the cover?

> EUGENE
> No. They did not.

> DAVID
> So, why are they neglecting you?

Eugene is not pleased. A pause. His cell pone rings. He
looks at it, turns it off.

> EUGENE
> As you can see I am a busy man, so let me
> get to the heart of the matter and tell
> you why I contacted you at this point in
> time. Father, you who are a novice, have
> just come into a fortune. Now believe me,
> this very minute as I speak, the sharks
> are circling the waters, the predators
> are poised to pounce, and they will
> devour you if you don't know how to
> defend yourself. And you don't, and I do.
> I am saying to you, let me handle your
> funds. Now why should you trust me? Not
> just because I am your son, but because I
> am a rich man. I have my own money, more
> than enough, I don't need yours, I don't
> want yours. For me there is no temptation
> to steal.

> DAVID
> So you are saying the rich should be
> trusted because they are rich?

> EUGENE
> Exactly.

                    DAVID
What an interesting concept. It is the
opposite of what I have always believed.

                    EUGENE
The more you think about it the more
you'll agree.

                    DAVID
Exactly. So that is what I will do, I
will think about it. And you must not
think for one moment that I do not
appreciate this great opportunity you are
affording me.

                    EUGENE
Excellent. But don't procrastinate.
Remember, time is of the essence, time is
of the essence.

                    DAVID
            (To Eve)
I told you he speaks like a lawyer.

Eugene hands David a business card.

                    EUGENE
Here's how to get in touch with me. Don't
delay. Nice to meet you, father.

He nods to the others and starts for the front door.
Steve accompanies him to let him out.

                    DAVID
You see, Eve, I have a son who is a
venture capitalist.

Steve returns to the room.

                    STEVE
            (To David)
Your son is some character.

                    DAVID
Maybe he is my biological son, but he is
not my son. You are not my biological
son, but you are my son. Please, now I
must speak to Eve.

Steve and Jane exit to their room. A long pause.

                    EVE
          I was deeply moved by what you just said
          to Stevie. And I could see that he was
          too.

                    DAVID
          I have never been good at expressing my
          true feelings. I see it now, where Stevie
          is concerned, I was too much of a critic
          and not enough of a helper. It is not so
          easy to bring up children.

                    EVE
          So I've discovered. David, you should
          rest now, you look extremely tired. So
          much excitement, one thing piled on
          another. And now with this latest...
          discovery, well, it's shocking.

                    DAVID
          This last bit of news, my son the venture
          capitalist, I don't think it has really
          registered on me yet. I have not absorbed
          it. But of one thing I am convinced, The
          Supreme Joker, up there in the heavens,
          has singled me out for special attention.

Eve tries to control her laughter.

                    EVE
          Well, I have to admit, you and Wanda,
          that is funny.

                    DAVID
          She is the only woman I ever had
          intercourse with and only one time.

                    EVE
          What? Why?

                    DAVID
          It was such hard work I decided I could
          do without it.

Eve is still trying to control her laughter, but not
succeeding.

                    DAVID (CONT'D)
          You see what I'm saying about the Supreme
          Joker singling me out? The only time I
          bought a lottery ticket, I won the
          jackpot. The only time I had sex, I
          fathered a child.
                    (MORE)

                    DAVID (CONT'D)
And the day I learned I won the jackpot,
I also got the results of medical tests
and learned I have only a short while to
live.

                    EVE
No!

                    DAVID
Yes, it's true.

                    EVE
Oh David!

                    DAVID
What can I say, there is no winning an
argument with the Supreme Joker. He
always gets the last word and the last
laugh.

                    EVE
Don't give up, David. The doctors are
often wrong about these things.

                    DAVID
We will see.

He rises.

                    DAVID (CONT'D)
Please don't tell anyone. Not yet.

                    EVE
Of course.

                    DAVID
Now I will take a nap.

DAVID starts to exit. At the door he turns to Eve.

                    DAVID (CONT'D)
Venture capitalists. I suppose they are
necessary.

He exits. She just sits there, devastated by what she has
just heard.

The lights fade. The lights rise on the living room.
Evening. Mature Eve, in a bathrobe and slippers is
sitting in an armchair. Younger David is seated nearby.

                    YOUNGER DAVID
If there is something you need, I am at
your service.

                    YOUNGER EVE
No thanks. You don't have to fuss over
me. David. It was just a simple outpatient procedure and I already feel back
to normal.

                    YOUNGER DAVID
But you must not deprive me of the chance
to be a noble caretaker.

                    YOUNGER EVE
Then let me direct you to another area.
At the hospital this morning I had to
sign a medical consent form. Well, you
know, that's routine. But then I brought
up the subject of a living will and
someone got me the forms to take home
with me. If it comes down to it, David,
if the situation should arise, I would
not want to be kept alive on life support
systems. I would like to designate you as
my representative, someone I've spoken to
who knows my wishes. Would that be all
right with you?

                    YOUNGER DAVID
Yes. I feel the same way about it. In
fact, if you have an extra set of forms.
I would like to designate you as my
representative. Will you agree to that?

                    YOUNGER EVE
I don't have extra forms but I do agree.

                    YOUNGER DAVID
Then we have accomplished something
important.

                    YOUNGER EVE
Not so fast. Now comes the really hard
part.

                    YOUNGER DAVID
Harder even than contemplating dying?

                    YOUNGER EVE
You might think so.

                    YOUNGER DAVID
You have piqued my interest.

                    YOUNGER EVE
This concerns Stevie... well, I don't
know how to approach this.
                      (MORE)

> YOUNGER EVE (CONT'D)
> You know my situation, my parents are
> dead, I was an only child, just like you,
> and I have no close living relatives.
> Stevie is only eleven and I've been
> putting this off, but I should really
> make a will appointing a guardian for
> Stevie in case, well you know, something
> happens to me. What I want to ask, would
> it be all right with you if I made you
> the executor of my will and appoint you
> Stevie's guardian?

A long pause.

> YOUNGER EVE (CONT'D)
> I know it's a lot to ask.

> YOUNGER DAVID
> I am afraid all I can offer for this job
> is a high level of incompetence.

> YOUNGER EVE
> I have confidence in you.

> YOUNGER DAVID
> But where is the evidence to support your
> judgment? I will do it, of course, but on
> certain conditions.

> YOUNGER EVE
> Oh?

> YOUNGER DAVID
> You must promise to follow a healthy
> lifestyle and not get hit by a truck.

> YOUNGER EVE
> I promise. Thank you so much, David.

She rises, bends over him, kisses him on the forehead. As
she bends over him the top flap of her robe parts. She
clutches it to close it, bends over and kisses him again.

> YOUNGER EVE (CONT'D)
> I think I will go to bed now. David,
> you're a sweetheart.

She exits.

> YOUNGER DAVID
> (Beaming)
> A sweetheart, no less.

The lights dim and come up on Eve, who is alone.

                    EVE (TO AUDIENCE)
So we had the brief but vital discussion
"contemplating dying" as David put it.
Well now, it is important to take some
time out from our busy schedules from
time to time to contemplate dying, don't
you think? After all, we're better able
to control the agenda on when to
contemplate, then when to die. Now some
news, we hadn't seen Eugene Kipnis again
since he decided to pop in on us the
first time. The reason, he's in jail.
I'll run through this as fast as I can.
When Eugene first visited us, he was
already under indictment. He was accused
of illegal practices that had enabled him
to amass his great fortune. Not that
Eugene didn't have many defenders who
insisted that his methods were not only
perfectly legal, but were actually
beneficial to the economy. Obviously, the
government was not in that camp, so
Eugene entered into a plea bargain with
the government in which he agreed to pay
millions in fines and make restitution of
millions. Eugene is now languishing in
one of those country club jails where the
guests are more apt to spend their time
playing bridge, or tennis, well ping-pong
anyway, than pumping iron. Ah, justice.
I've come to learn in David's life, and I
suppose mine too, events tend to occur
with a certain symmetry.

The phone rings. Eve answers.

                    EVE (CONT'D)
Hello. In jail? Oh, God! .... Drugs? That
boy is killing me. David did? He went
out? I assumed he was in his room. I've
been home about half an hour. Will you be
home soon? Thanks, Jane.

Stunned, Eve replaces the phone.

                    EVE (CONT'D)
Shit! Shit! Shit! Shit!

Very agitated, she paces the room for a while. She pours
herself a drink from a bottle in her liquor cabinet. She
sits and drinks and waits. After a while, David enters
form the front door. He is using he cane again and really
relying on it now. He looks terrible. He sees Eve.

                    DAVID
        You know?

                    EVE
        I know.

Wearily, he sits.

                    EVE(CONT'D)
        You shouldn't have gone out.

                    DAVID
        I had to go. I took a taxi. When was the
        last time I was in a taxi? When I was
        born and my parents brought me home from
        the hospital? Maybe two or three times
        since.

                    EVE
        Are you all right?

                    DAVID
        This is a question better left unasked.

                    EVE
        I'm sorry you had to get involved.

                    DAVID
        There is no way for me to not be
        involved. You know Eve, I have been
        thinking about Harry a lot, lately.
        Harry, I don't have to tell you, was a
        good person, a sensitive person, but he
        was also a strong person. A very firm
        person. With Harry's strong presence I
        don't think any of this would have
        happened.

                    EVE
        Who knows? Sometimes nothing helps.

                    DAVID
        I went to the bail bond office. His bail
        was ten thousand dollars and the fee is a
        little more than one thousand dollars...

                    EVE
        I'll pay you back...

                    DAVID
        Please, Eve, don't insult me. I am not
        talking to you about money, I am sharing
        my experience with you.
                    (MORE)

                    DAVID (CONT'D)
Never in my life did I imagine I would
have anything to do with obtaining a bail
bond. It was a very strange experience
for me. It was like a dream and I kept
asking myself, What am I doing in a place
like this?

                    EVE
Thank you for taking care of it.

                    DAVID
Where is Jane?

                    EVE
She just called. She'll be here any
minute.

                    DAVID
She didn't want me to get him out on
bail.

                    EVE
Oh?

                    DAVID
She said we have to stop coddling him...
all of us.

                    EVE
She's probably right.

                    DAVID
Today is Friday, without bail now he had
no chance to get out until the
arraignment Monday morning.

                    EVE
Maybe a weekend in jail would have taught
him a lesson.

                    DAVID
From what I understand, he didn't like
the accommodations. And he complained
bitterly about the class of people in the
cell with him. Drunks, some covered with
vomit, and they fight among themselves. I
suppose it could be dangerous.

                    EVE
You're a softy. When will he be released?

> DAVID
> They said at the bail bond office it
> could take a couple hours for the paper
> work.

> EVE
> Where is the jail? I'll get him.

> DAVID
> Wait. Wait for Jane.

Sounds are heard at the front. Jane enters. David
gestures saying, "see I was right." She goes directly to
Eve and they hug. Wearily, she sits.

> JANE
> I thought there was a rule that an
> arrestee was entitled to only one phone
> call. He kept calling, he must have
> called a dozen times. He's a pain in the
> butt even when he's in jail.

> EVE
> Does he have a cell phone?

> JANE
> Just a pay phone in the holding cell.
> Most of the time he called collect. My
> boss was not amused.

> EVE
> Maybe I should go get him now?

> JANE
> I checked, he was released a while ago.

> EVE
> How will he...

> JANE
> Don't worry, his car isn't that far from
> the jail. He can walk it. He wanted me to
> pick him up at the station. When we got
> to his car, he wanted to show me that the
> dashboard "low fuel" light was on. He
> wanted me to follow him to the gas
> station to be there while he filled his
> tank. All of this is his explanation as
> to why he got off the freeway in a known
> drug area. He had to, don't you see,
> because he was low on gas. He insists
> he's innocent.

                    EVE
                 (To Jane)
          Do you believe him?

                    JANE
          No. Do you?

                    EVE
          No.

                    DAVID
          I also cast a "no" vote.

Sounds are heard at the front door. Steve enters.

                    STEVE
          Hi.

                    EVE
          Well look what the cat dragged in.

                    STEVE
          I didn't do anything. (Turns to Jane) Why
          didn't you meet me? I could have proved
          to you I was out of gas and that's why I
          had to get off the freeway in that
          neighborhood.

                    JANE
          You explained that on the phone a bunch
          of times.

                    EVE
          Why don't you tell us exactly what
          happened?

                    STEVE
          I was just about to run out of gas, so I
          got off the freeway. The gas station was
          just a block down the street so I was
          going to get gas and get back on the
          freeway. I was waiting at the light when
          this guy came up on the passenger side.
          It didn't feel right, so I raised the
          window. The light changed, I drove about
          a quarter of a block and the cops stopped
          me. It turned out they were doing a
          sting. They searched me, they searched
          the car, they didn't find anything. I'm
          sure they were gonna let me go and then
          one of the cops asked me if I had ever
          been arrested. There was no reason for me
          to lie, so I told him yes. Anyhow, that's
          when they arrested me.
                    (MORE)

                    STEVE (CONT'D)
Look, this is a bad arrest, I didn't do
anything, I'm sure they'll drop the whole
thing at the arraignment.

                    JANE
I wish I shared your confidence.

                    STEVE
But I didn't do anything. I told you
exactly what happened.

                    JANE
You didn't tell us why they arrested you.

                    STEVE
It was a mistake! They searched me, they
searched my car, they didn't find
anything. I'll take a lie detector test!

                    JANE
Bullshit! If you were a black guy or a
Latino, and the cops arrested you, I'd
buy it, but a nice clean cut white guy?
Why would they bother you without a
reason? Come on, get real.

                    STEVE
They didn't find anything because I
didn't do anything.

                    JANE
I talked to the desk sergeant on the
phone. He was very talkative. He said
when they do these things, they slip
plastic bags containing macadamia nuts in
lieu of drugs to the purchasers in
exchange for fifty dollars.

                    STEVE
Macadamia nuts, you're nuts!

                    JANE
Then let me tell you about another nutty
thing. Today I discovered there was fifty
dollars missing from my wallet. Now let
me surmise where that fifty dollars wound
up. I surmise that fifty dollars is in
the arrest file of a certain individual
who purchased some Macadamia nuts. (She
rises) I'm out of here.

She strides to her room... Steve looks on unable to
respond. Eve rises.

                        EVE
          Jane...

Eve follows Jane to her room. Steve and David remain
seated.

                        STEVE
          I didn't take her money.

                        DAVID
                (Mocking)
          It was a coincidence.

                        STEVE
          You don't have to be sarcastic.

                        DAVID
          You would deny me a little sarcasm in my
          old age?

A long Pause.

                        STEVE
          Thanks for bailing me out. I appreciate
          it.

                        DAVID
          You are not sincere, you are not honest.

                        STEVE
          I swear to God I didn't attempt to buy
          drugs and I didn't steal Jane's money!

                        DAVID
          Liar. LIAR! You are an enemy of the
          truth. You are a parasite, a destroyer of
          life. You love no one, you care for no
          one, you suck the marrow from our bones
          while we are all still alive. Liar!
          Thief! Enemy!

He is brandishing his cane when Eve and Jane come rushing
into the room.

                        EVE
          David, David...

They are restraining him and supporting him at the same
time.

BLACKOUT

Lights up on Eve.

                         EVE (TO AUDIENCE) (CONT'D)
Under a new, enlightened California law,
Stevie was able to choose drug treatment
rather than jail time. He wanted to live
at home during treatment but I refused. I
insisted he spend time in a drug
residence for recovering addicts. They're
dreadful places and I thought he needed
that experience. However, I did persuade
Jane not to leave. So since he has
pledged to stay straight, he exacted a
promise from me to give up my little
alcohol habit. Well, he had a point,
didn't he? As for DAVID, clearly he was
not doing well.

David enters from his room. He is in a wheelchair.

                         DAVID
I have made arrangements to enter a
hospice.

                         EVE
You don't have to, you know. This is your
home.

                         DAVID
It is not simple.

                         EVE
It doesn't need to be simple. If it's
complicated, then it's complicated. If
you need a full time professional
caregiver, there is ample space here.
David, I am sure you prefer to remain
here and this is where you should be. I
want you here.

                         DAVID
I know you are sincere and I appreciate
your offer. But, Eve, I must do it my
way. "Do it my way?" I sound like Frank
Sinatra.

DAVID chuckles at his joke.

                         EVE
But why?

                         DAVID
You know I went to see the hospice. It is
very nice... welcoming. I saw my room, it
is attractive. From it, I look out to a
beautiful garden.
                         (MORE)

                    DAVID (CONT'D)
And there is also a wood deck with
reclining chairs. Now that I saw it, I
have this fantasy that at night I will be
on an ocean cruise on a luxury boat and I
will be tucked in very snugly in my
lounge chair on the deck looking up at
the sky filled with stars. It is such a
happy feeling. Of course, nowadays the
night sky from a big city does not afford
a view of many stars, but I know they are
there and I will use my imagination to
see them. We must do something about
pollution.

                    EVE
Oh, David...

                    DAVID
Listen, Eve, before I leave for the
hospice I wish to say goodbye to Jane and
Stevie and to you. Once I am there I
don't wish any further contact of any
kind.

                    EVE
          (Stunned)
Are you sure?

                    DAVID
My mind is made up.

                    EVE
When are you leaving?

                    DAVID
The day after tomorrow.

                    EVE
I'll make sure Jane and Stevie are here
tomorrow night.

The lights dim. Eve exits. The lights go up partially.
The following is played in a half light. David is in his
wheelchair. Jane enters and sits near David. She holds
his hand for awhile. David extracts a larger manila
envelope from the space between his side and the arm of
the chair. He hands it to Jane.

                    JANE
Oh, is that your...

                    DAVID
...My masterpiece.

                    JANE
You finished it.

                    DAVID
With no time to spare.

                    JANE
And this is for me?

                    DAVID
Of course. Read it when you can. Since I
will not ask you if you liked it, you are
spared the necessity of lying to me or
being diplomatically evasive. The best
policy, I think, is to never allow
yourself to be put in the position of
reading someone's manuscript.

                    JANE
Yes.

                    DAVID
On the other hand, if you like it,
perhaps you can send me some kind of
telephathic message. I will be on the
alert to receive it.

                    JANE
I'll concentrate very hard.

                    DAVID
I wish you every success in life. I can't
express with words my admiration for
you... no, not just admiration... love.

She embraces him. The lights dim further. Jane exits.
Steve enters, sits near David. A long silence.

                    STEVE
Are you afraid?

                    DAVID
Afraid? Of what?

                    STEVE
Afraid to die.

                    DAVID
No. I am not afraid to die.

                    STEVE
I thought everyone was. I am.

                    DAVID
Perhaps you have observed, I am somewhat
different.

                    STEVE
Well...

                    DAVID
Steve, you notice I am addressing you as
Steve and not Stevie. I am trying to
confer a sense of manhood on you that you
have not yet achieved on your own.

                    STEVE
I don't think I ...

                    DAVID
What I am saying is that it's time for
you to grow up and start acting like a
man, an adult. You must take
responsibility for your life. What you
do. Nobody can do that for you.

                    STEVE
I know.

                    DAVID
So...

                    STEVE
The need to use... I can't control it.
It's like I'm a slave to it.

                    DAVID
Then you must emancipate yourself.

                    STEVE
I'm trying.

                    DAVID
I think I should have spent more time
telling you about your father. He was a
wonderful man. Full of life and he had
strength of character. We were best
friends. Why he wanted to be my friend,
I'm not so sure. He knew that I was a
little strange. Sometimes he would make
little jokes about me. In a gentle way.
But if somebody else tried it. No way. He
protected me. It was his nature to
protect the underdog. He would fight for
what he believed was right. You have
inherited his genes too, remember that.

                    STEVE
I will.

                    DAVID
I'm sorry I couldn't be a better father
to you.

                    STEVE
I'm sorry I couldn't be a better son.

                    DAVID
So I am sorry and you are sorry. We are
both sorry. Now, go out and make a good
life for yourself.

They embrace. The lights dim. Steve exits. Eve enters.
They sit in silence.

                    DAVID (CONT'D)
Stevie... maybe he should be called *Steve*
now. I am sure he will give up drugs.

                    EVE
I hope so.

                    DAVID
And maybe it's time you stopped with the
alcoholic refreshments.

                    EVE
I have wondered why you never mentioned
it to me.

                    DAVID
I thought I would, as they say, cut you
some slack. Living with me in the same
house must have been very stressful.

                    EVE
Well, yes, at times, but I can't give you
all the credit.

                    DAVID
Like every long relationship there were
difficult times and there were good
times.

                    EVE
Yes, like that new year's eve when we
danced.

                    DAVID
          (Correcting her)
When we almost danced.

                    EVE
          Yes, we almost danced.

They fall silent.

                    DAVID
          I can't thank you enough.

                    EVE
          For what?

                    DAVID
          For everything. You gave me a life. On my
          own I could do nothing. You gave me a
          home, a family. Who else would put up
          with me?

                    EVE
          No, that's not true.

                    DAVID
          It is true. Eve, I am not without
          insight. There was always something wrong
          with me, with my brain. It did not
          function normally. The neurons were
          misfiring? The serotonin was not in
          balance? Something kept me from
          functioning. Probably it was genetic and
          could not be helped. Who knows?

                    EVE
          I don't agree with any of that. Maybe,
          you're a little... eccentric, I'll give
          you that.

                    DAVID
          Eccentric. I like that word. No, it was
          more. I could not participate fully in
          life, I was not a participator.

                    EVE
          Participant, I think, is the word you
          want.

                    DAVID
          No, no, participator, it has a stronger,
          more active sound than participant. Let
          me coin this word, at least, if it is not
          already a word.

                    EVE
          Alright, I won't insist especially since
          you're right.

> DAVID
>
> I hope I wasn't too much trouble.

> EVE
>
> We lived like husband and wife, except
> for the sex.

> DAVID
>
> For you, I should have made the effort.

They kiss, embrace. He clings to her. The lights fade to
black.

Lights up. Eve enters.

> EVE (TO AUDIENCE)
>
> I spoke with someone at the hospice every
> day. Clearly, they were good people. The
> reports about David were uniform, He was
> serene, happy even. He died six weeks
> from the day he entered. (a beat) I said
> early on he was a boring man, well, not
> so boring. No, not at all. Like most
> people, I suppose, there was more than
> meets the eye. I guess I realized it on
> some level, because I... well, I always
> tried to.. Well.. Okay, what about
> David's fortune? I know you're curious.
> And don't make any assumptions. No
> lottery jackpot has ever been spent this
> way in the past, and probably never will
> again. Let me now tell you about the
> David Kipnis Foundation. It provides for
> the acquisition of a suitable property
> and the construction of a three hundred
> seat state of the art theatre to be known
> as *The Kipnis*. Alongside it will be a
> separate ninety seat theatre to be known
> as *The David*. Whenever possible,
> admission will be free or at a nominal
> cost. On the same property there will be
> constructed a separate building which
> will be knows as *The David Kipnis Center
> for the Prevention and Treatment of Drug
> Addiction*. Oh, the chairperson of the
> board of directors of the David Kipnis
> foundation is yours truly. Jane Cousins
> is also a named director and an assistant
> artistic director. Oh, let me tell you
> about David's play. Jane loved it. We had
> it evaluated by "experts" who used such
> adjectives as witty, charming,
> delightful.
>
> (MORE)

                    EVE (TO AUDIENCE) (CONT'D)
So David's play *The Death of a Tailor*
will open the *The David* when it is
completed. Also, we have been in touch
with the publishers of Arthur Miller's
The Death of a Salesman and they are
definitely interested in allowing us to
open *The Kipnis* with *The Death of a
Salesman.*

She catches her breath.

                    EVE (CONT'D)
Wheeewww. There's so much and I'm just
giving you the barest details. Now about
Eugene Kipnis, remember him? He's still
in jail, but he seems happy. He stays in
touch with me. He, too, is writing a
play, it must be in the genes. His
working title is *The Confessions of a
Venture Capitalist.* He says it is of
necessity, a very long play. Of course,
if it has merit, we know of a suitable
venue for it's production. By the way,
Eugene loves the idea of the David Kipnis
Foundation. He would like to associate
himself with it and be helpful in any way
he can. Since he'll still have a few
billion dollars in pocket change left
over... welcome. Oh, he has mentioned
funding a think tank. *The Eugene Kipnis
Center for the examination of Ethics and
Morality in Business.* It will also
examine such subjects as the failure of
capitalism to eliminate poverty even in
unprecedented, sustained periods of
prosperity. Not the usual subject matter
of conservative think tanks, is it? And
it certainly would have made his father
proud. Now about Stevie... *Steve.* He took
David's death harder than anyone. It has
been slow going for him. But he is
remaining off drugs. And he will soon be
resuming his college studies. He is, of
course, a beneficiary of David's will,
but only if he completes college and
remains drug free for five years. I feel
confident. He and Jane are no longer an
item. But they are not hostile.

She enters the kitchen, returns with a cocktail glass
containing a pinkish liquid.

                    EVE (CONT'D)
At the beginning, I said I was going to
tell you the story of David Kipnis. But I
have also told you my story, haven't I?
Because our lives were so inextricably
entwined.

She sips her drink.

                    EVE (CONT'D)
This is a cocktail. It's Cranberry juice.
I don't drink alcohol anymore.

She sips again.

                    EVE (CONT'D)
Not bad. And it's good for the bladder.

She salutes the audience with her drink, then exits.

END OF PLAY

UNTITLED BY SCOTT LIPSHITZ

CHARACTERS:

Sofia Gold - About 40

June Priest - About 30

Scott Lipshitz - About 30

Max Gold - About 45

Alistair Cross - About 30

The set is a stage, bare but for a table and some chairs
upstage. No backdrop. Additional playing areas, which
should be depicted as minimally as possible, are: the
office shared by Sofia and June; Sofia's living room;
Max's living room; a booth in a restaurant: a park bench.
Sofia enters. She addresses the audience directly.

> SOFIA
> (to audience)
> It came over the transom, as we say in
> our business, meaning of course, it was
> not submitted on a recommendation or eve
> preceded by a query letter. Usually, we
> give short shrift to such submissions
> since we have made it known to the
> Dramatists Guild and all Writer's Market
> publications we will not read unsolicited
> manuscripts. In this case, there was even
> a bit of a mystery about it since it had
> not come in the mail. It was just there
> one morning on June's desk, strange
> because June and I always lock the door
> when we leave the office unattended. But
> there it was in a crisp, new manila
> envelope somehow waiting, demanding even,
> to be opened. Inside, a standard
> manuscript, and on the cover where the
> title customarily appears it said:
> "Untitled by Scott Lipshitz," posing the
> question as to whether this writer with
> the unfortunate surname had not yet
> decided on a title or whether the title
> was in fact, "Untitled."

June enters.

                              JUNE
                        (to the audience)
          I can't explain it, really I can't. I'm
          not one of these New Age people who
          believe in alternative everything. Maybe
          they could explain it, I couldn't. All I
          knew is that there was something very
          strange about my reaction to finding the
          manuscript in the center of my desk, the
          racing heart, the breathlessness. It was
          a reaction that bore no logical
          relationship to the event. The envelope
          was addressed to Sofia, only her name -
          Sofia Gold, appeared on it and nothing
          more.

JUNE crosses to SOFIA who is now sitting at her desk.

                         JUNE (CONT'D)
          This was addressed to you.

SOFIA looks at it without accepting it.

                              SOFIA
          So, don't you open the mail anymore?

                              JUNE
          It's a manuscript, I'm sure.

                              SOFIA
          What else? Open it.

JUNE starts to open the envelope with a letter opener.

                         SOFIA (CONT'D)
          Wait a minute, what's this yellow stuff?

                              JUNE
          I don't know.

SOFIA takes the envelope from JUNE and sniffs on the
spot.

                              SOFIA
          I think it's mustard.

She hands the envelope back to JUNE who opens it and
removes a manuscript.

                              JUNE
          The writer's name is Scott Lipshitz.

                         SOFIA
                    (grimaces)
          Never heard of him. Have you?

                         JUNE
          No.

                         SOFIA
          Then send it back. Or chuck it for all I
          care.

                         JUNE
          Chuck it?

                         SOFIA
          Yes.

                         JUNE
          You've never chucked a manuscript in your
          life.

                         SOFIA
          But I've been sorely tempted. Maybe now
          is the time to begin.

                         JUNE
                    (protectively)
          I'm going to read it tonight.

                         SOFIA
          Suit yourself.

     JUNE exits with the manuscript.

                         SOFIA (CONT'D)
          And that, believe it or not, was the
          beginning of the beginning. As it turned
          out, if I many leap ahead a bit, Scott He-
          of-the-unfortunate-surname, was not
          exactly waiting at the telephone for our
          response.

     Enter JUNE - open area.

                         JUNE
                    (to audience)
          I knew, I knew at once. I hadn't finished
          the first page and I knew. How? I don't
          know, that's part of the mystery, isn't
          it? I read it at home that night at one
          sitting, and when I finished there was
          not the slightest doubt in my mind that
          it was a masterpiece.
                    (MORE)

                         JUNE (CONT'D)
          Ecstatic, I telephoned Sofia and told her
          my reaction. She knew I was a tough
          critic, she trusted my evaluations and
          she promised to read it first thing in
          the morning. The following morning she
          kept her nose in the manuscript until she
          had finished.

Lights change. SOFIA, now at her desk, looks up and
places the manuscript on her desk. JUNE observes her.

                         JUNE (CONT'D)
          Well?

                         SOFIA
          It's pretty good.

                         JUNE
          Pretty good?

                         SOFIA
          Yeah, it's okay.

                         JUNE
          Okay? Just okay?

                         SOFIA
          It had merit.

                         JUNE
          Merit. Is that all you can...

                         SOFIA
          All right. It's brilliant. In fact, I
          truly believe it's a *Masterpiece.*

                      JUNE & SOFIA
          It's a masterpiece.

They hold hands and being to dance in a circle.

                      JUNE & SOFIA (CONT'D)
          It's a masterpiece, it's a masterpiece,
          it's a master...

SOFIA breaks off.

                         SOFIA
          Oh, my God. Suppose he's been making
          multiple submissions...

                         JUNE
          ...Should I try to reach...

                    SOFIA
          I'll do it now. The manuscript, his
          telephone number's on the cover.

She refers to the manuscript and dials the number.

                    SOFIA (CONT'D)
          I'll put it on speaker.

After several rings are heard:

                    SCOTT'S VOICE
          This is Scott, leave your number.

Beep.

                    SOFIA
               (businesslike)
          This is Sofia Gold. I've read your play.
          Please call 212.374.3190, when it's
          convenient.

She hangs up.

                    JUNE
          When it's convenient?

                    SOFIA
          Sure. We don't want the fellow to get
          conceited.

                    JUNE
          But, we want the first shot at him.

                    SOFIA
          Of course, but never forget, every writer
          is a royal pain in the ass. We don't want
          to start off by encouraging him too much.
          And if we do meet him, try not to be too
          worshipful.

                    JUNE
               (hurt)
          I'll try to act professionally.

                    SOFIA
          You always do. But, in this case your
          enthusiasm, it seems, has no bounds. Very
          uncharacteristic, I might add.

                    JUNE
          A moment ago, you weren't so very laid-
          back yourself.

                         SOFIA
          True. But now, normalcy has returned.

                         JUNE
          Oh, it has?

JUNE turns away.

                         JUNE (CONT'D)
                    (to audience)
          My mind was a jumble of thoughts, perhaps
          verging on insanity because I had to
          consider whether or not I had fallen in
          love with this playwright. How could such
          a thing even be conceivable? I knew
          nothing about him. Was he old? Was he
          young? Was he single? Was he involved?
          Was he married? Was he good looking, was
          he ugly, was he a mensch or was he a
          louse? But on the last point I had the
          evidence of his play, you see, and I knew
          its creator could only be a noble spirit.
          A further consolation, I had heard his
          voice on the answering machine and it
          was, in my estimation, the voice of a
          younger man, and somehow I had decided a
          pleasant looking man. Although I didn't
          speak about any of this with Sofia she
          understood, I'm certain, and as I was
          beginning to learn she was not without a
          cruel streak.

                         SOFIA
                    (to June)
          Of course, you can't really tell what a
          man looks like from his telephone voice.
          My guess is that our playwright is about
          forty, thin and stooped, with balding,
          kinky hair and eye glasses with coke-
          bottom lenses. I imagine he is about as
          prepossessing as say Woody Allen.

                         JUNE
          Time will tell. I contacted the
          Dramatists Guild, he's not a member, not
          even an associate member. I checked all
          the area phone books, and information,
          he's not listed. Shouldn't we try to
          contact him again

                         SOFIA
          No.

                        JUNE
          Maybe he didn't get the message. Maybe
          his answering machine malfunctioned.

                        SOFIA
          And maybe it wasn't necessary for us to
          contact him at all. After all, he was
          resourceful enough to have his manuscript
          placed on your desk. I'm betting we'll
          hear from him when he's ready without our
          running after him.

                        JUNE
          I guess I'm not good at playing games.
          And in this instance I don't even see the
          need for it.

JUNE exits the office area.

                        SOFIA
                    (to audience)
          I think I was being perverse about this.
          I sensed June's inner white heat of
          excitement about this writer and his play
          and somehow it seemed to diminish mine a
          bit. And to some extent I did regret my
          initial reaction in contacting Mr.
          Lipshitz right away. I've been an agent
          for many years and as much as I'd like to
          discover and launch a major new writer
          I've learned to be somewhat fatalistic
          about it occurring. It will happen if it
          will happen. Let the Machiavellian types
          plot their plots, I'll just go on as
          always.

                        JUNE
                    (to audience)
          As it happened I was spending the
          afternoon at the dentist's getting a root
          canal when Scott made his first
          appearance at our office and I had to
          rely on Sofia for an account of what took
          place. Needless to say, I'd have been
          there, despite my toothache, if I'd known
          he was coming.

SOFIA is at her desk reading, SCOTT, thirtyish, enters.
He raps on the open door. She looks up.

                        SCOTT
          I'm Scott Lipshitz. I thought I...

                    SOFIA
          Oh, Mr. Lipshitz...

                    SCOTT
          ...drop by to see if you have any news
          for me.

                    SOFIA
          I'm Sofia Gold. It's always better if you
          call first for an appointment.

                    SCOTT
          Yeah? Okay, I'll go now and call you for
          an appointment. Unless you got a few
          minutes now.

                    SOFIA
          Sit down, Mr. Lipshitz.

He sits.

                    SCOTT
          You can call me Scott.

                    SOFIA
          Okay, Scott. My assistant, June Priest,
          read your play and was very enthusiastic
          about it. She gave it to me to read, and
          I, too, think it's an excellent work.

                    SCOTT
          Yeah, so what happens next?

                    SOFIA
          That's the question all right. We'll
          discuss that but first tell me a little
          about yourself.

                    SCOTT
          Uh, well, I really don't like talking
          about myself.

                    SOFIA
          Oh? We will need to know about your
          writing background.

                    SCOTT
          How come?

                    SOFIA
          People we would be contacting about your
          play will want to know. It would create a
          negative impression if all we can answer
          is 'duh...'

                         SCOTT
          You could tell them I want to be
          anonymous.

                         SOFIA
          Yes, we could.

A Beat

                         SOFIA (CONT'D)
          Let me be blunt, I want to know something
          about you. Is that acceptable?

                         SCOTT
          Yeah, sure, you ask, I'll answer.

                         SOFIA
          Have you ever had a play produced?

                         SCOTT
          No.

                         SOFIA
          Anywhere, no matter how tiny the venue?

                         SCOTT
          No.

                         SOFIA
          Ever had a staged reading anywhere, this
          play or anything else?

                         SCOTT
          No.

                         SOFIA
          Do you write in any other genres?

SCOTT hesitates, possibly confused

                         SOFIA (CONT'D)
          Such as short stories, novels,
          screenplays?

                         SCOTT
          No.

                         SOFIA
          Do you belong to a theatre group?

                         SCOTT
          No.

                        SOFIA
Ever?

                        SCOTT
No.

                        SOFIA
Have you ever studied plays? Taken course
in play writing in a college or
elsewhere?

                        SCOTT
No.

                        SOFIA
How many plays have you written?

                        SCOTT
This is it.

                        SOFIA
Your one and only play?

                        SCOTT
My one and only.

                        SOFIA
Then it's really remarkable, your writing
at this level. Have you submitted the
play elsewhere?

                        SCOTT
No.

                        SOFIA
Contacted any other agent?

                        SCOTT
No.

                        SOFIA
How did you happen to pick me?

                        SCOTT
A hunch.

                        SOFIA
A hunch?

                        SCOTT
Yeah. I went to the library and found
your name in a directory of agents who
handle playwrights. I picked you.

                    SOFIA
Why me?

                    SCOTT
A hunch?

                    SOFIA
Oh?

                    SCOTT
Once I went to Las Vegas. I went into a
giant casino, walked past hundreds of
slot machines, stopped at one, played it,
and on my first play hit a $10,000
jackpot. I play hunches, doesn't
everybody... sometimes?

                    SOFIA
Besides hitting jackpots, how do you
support yourself?

                    SCOTT
I was born with a silver spoon in my
mouth.

                    SOFIA
You could have fooled me.

SCOTT laughs

                    SCOTT
I work at whatever comes along. I don't
exactly live high on the hog. How long
does it take to do something with a play?
(She shrugs) A ball park figure?

                    SOFIA
Who the hell knows?

SCOTT rises, turns to leave.

                    SCOTT
Okay...

                    SOFIA
Do you want me to represent you?

                    SCOTT
Sure, I told you.

                    SOFIA
All right, I've got some papers for you
to sign, and we need to talk more. Sit
down again.

He sits. She removes papers from a desk drawer and shoves them across the desk.

                    SOFIA (CONT'D)
          I've never said this to a new client
          before, but I feel impelled to say it to
          you. Please don't be a pain in the ass.

                    SCOTT
          Hey, maybe you'll learn to love me.

                    JUNE
          Sofia gave me her impressions of their
          meeting. She said he was thirtyish, not
          bad looking. She didn't ask, but she
          guessed he was single. Overall, she
          thought he was kind of strange, and
          certainly stingy with information about
          himself. He didn't, according to her,
          exactly ooze sincerity, but on reflection
          she thought maybe that was because he
          really was being entirely honest. Figure
          that out.

                    SOFIA
                 (to audience)
          No doubt about it, he was not your
          typical, earnest young writer. He was a
          man, I thought, who wore many masks to
          hide his true self. Thinking of how June
          would react to him, and for some reason I
          kept putting myself in June's mind where
          Scott was concerned, I was sure she would
          fall for him completely and was just as
          sure he would break her heart. But for me
          this was a time for action. Mr.
          Lipshitz's play, I was convinced, was a
          masterpiece, therefore it deserved a
          Broadway production, normally an
          impossibility for an unknown writer. But
          I had a secret weapon, my dear cousin Max
          Gold, who was very fond of me and who was
          very, very, very, very, very, very rich.
          My plan, I would invite him to be one of
          the backers of the production I was
          envisioning and start the ball rolling.

MAX GOLD enters. He is about forty-five.

                        MAX
                   (to audience)
          I always had time for Sofia, my favorite
          relative, so when she called and
          suggested we get together for lunch, I
          was agreeable. She didn't lose much time
          in getting to the point.

MAX crosses to a restaurant booth where SOFIA is seated,
waiting. They hug. He sits opposite her.

                        SOFIA
          I'm representing a new playwright whose
          play, I believe, is a masterpiece. I want
          to produce it, a Broadway production.

                        MAX
          Is that a conflict of interest for you to
          be his agent and producer?

                        SOFIA
          It can be arranged, legally and
          ethically.

                        MAX
          Okay.

                        SOFIA
          The playwright's name is Scott Lipshitz.

                        MAX
          I'll try not hold that against him

A BEAT

                        MAX (CONT'D)
          And June, does she share your opinion of
          Mr. Lipshitz?

                        SOFIA
          Even more so.

                        MAX
          Even more so.

                        SOFIA
          Max, if you're willing to come on board
          as an investor, I'm sure I'll be able to
          attract other backers.

                        MAX
          What's a ballpark figure for the entire
          production?

                         SOFIA
          For a Broadway play, it could go up to
          ten million.

                         MAX
          Okay, forget about the other backers,
          I'll finance the whole enchilada.

SOFIA is speechless, her mouth agape. She remains that
way for the remainder of the scene. MAX turns away from
SOFIA.

                         MAX (CONT'D)
                    (to audience)
          I realize I'd dropped a little bombshell,
          but what's the point of being 'rich' if
          you can't indulge yourself on occasion
          like that? And, I didn't mind having my
          name associated with an artistic
          endeavor. I did explain to Sofia,
          however, that I did not have time to get
          too involved with her project. I don't
          think she minded.

He plants a kiss of her forehead and exits.

                         SOFIA
                    (to audience)
          I recommend that everyone have at least
          one doting relative who is also
          fabulously rich.

Lights down on Sofia. Up on June.

                         JUNE
                    (to audience)
          Plans for the production were moving
          ahead and I still hadn't met Scott. I
          knew we would have many opportunities to
          meet in the future yet somehow I felt
          left out of things, but then soon after,
          he became a regular visitor...at
          lunchtime.

She works at her desk. SCOTT enters. She looks up.

                         SCOTT
          I'm Scott.

                         JUNE
                    (flustered)
          I'm June Priest...

JUNE extends her hand to shake and starts to rise

                    SCOTT
          You don't have to get up.

An awkward silence

                    JUNE
          I read your play, I loved it.

                    SCOTT
          Yeah, Sofia told me. So, where are we
          now?

                    JUNE
          With your play?

                    SCOTT
          Yeah, what happens next?

                    JUNE
          We're searching for a director.

                    SCOTT
          Is that hard?

                    JUNE
          It's very important, we want the best.

SCOTT nods approvingly.

                    JUNE (CONT'D)
          Sofia won't be in the rest of the day.

                    SCOTT
          I know. Well, I suppose you're getting
          ready to go to lunch.

                    JUNE
          Yes. Sometimes I order from the deli, but
          today's so lovely I thought I'd go out.
          Would you care to join me?

                    SCOTT
          Yeah, but I gotta tell you up front I'm
          kind of broke.

                    JUNE
          Oh, that's not a problem.

                    SCOTT
          Okay.

They exit. Lights dim. Up on Sofia.

                    SOFIA
                 (to audience)
     Scott and June became regular luncheon
     companions, understandable since he would
     usually show up at the office just before
     lunchtime. I permitted June to have a
     clear field with Scott for lunch.
     Noblesse oblige. Well, Scott soon began
     popping up at my apartment at dinner
     time, and therein hangs a tale.

                    JUNE
                 (to audience)
     Our lunches together soon became routine.
     There was never again a reference to
     money , part of the routine was that I
     paid. I know Scott did receive some
     option money for his play but I suppose
     he had preexisting debts that absorbed
     it. Anyhow, he never seemed uncomfortable
     about money matters. Our time together
     was rather strange, Scott just didn't
     talk very much. He almost never initiated
     a conversation, and when I did he made
     the shortest possible reply and never
     allowed it to develop into a true
     exchange. It was frustrating and at times
     I'd experience a surge of anger about his
     maddening refusal to communicate, but I
     internalized it. I tried discussing his
     play, here I was sure we would find a
     common ground, but he made it clear that
     this, more than anything, was forbidden
     territory. Yet, I liked being with him,
     wanted to be with him very much, in fact,
     at times felt near euphoria just being in
     his presence. Later I learned he was also
     a regular visitor, for dinner, at Sofia's
     place and the first time he appeared
     there it was unexpected.

Lights dim and up on Sofia. We hear the sound of door
chimes. SOFIA'S apartment. SOFIA is admitting SCOTT.

                    SOFIA
                 (surprised)
     Oh, Scott...

                    SCOTT
     Hi. I thought I'd come by.

                    SOFIA
     How did you learn where I live?

                         SCOTT
          I have ways of finding out things.

                         SOFIA
          Oh? Okay. Come in.

They sit. An awkward silence.

                         SOFIA (CONT'D)
          Anything in particular you want to see me
          about?

                         SCOTT
          Uh...the play, how's it coming?

                         SOFIA
          As you know, we've formed a production
          company. It's well funded, I'm happy to
          say. Right now the search is on for a
          director. And if you have any ideas you
          want to share with us, feel free. In
          theatre, as I've explained to you,
          writers have a lot of power.

                         SCOTT
          I'll let you know if I think of
          something. (He sniffs the air) Something
          smells good.

                         SOFIA
          Dinner's on the stove. There's plenty if
          you...

                         SCOTT
          Great!

                         SOFIA
          I'll have to check, in a few minutes.

A BEAT

                         SCOTT
          You're a good looking woman.

                         SOFIA
          Thank you for the compliment.

                         SCOTT
          You're a sexy woman too.

                         SOFIA
          Sexy, no less?

                    SCOTT
Very sexy.

                    SOFIA
Why, Scott, don't tell me you lust for
me.

                    SCOTT
I guess that's what I'm telling you.
Something like that.

He places his hand fully on her right breast.

                    SOFIA
Take you hand away!

He removes his hand. Furiously, she slaps his face.

                    SCOTT
Wow, you hit hard.

                    SOFIA
Don't you ever do that again.

His eyes are locked on hers, impudently, as he slowly
returns his hand to her breast and keeps it there. For a
moment her expression registers astonishment and rage,
then it fades and in a moment she begins to laugh. It
develops into a paroxysm of laughter and after a while
Scott joins in the laughter.

Lights fade on Sofia and Scott as Max enters.

                    MAX
                (to audience)
So, I'm a meshuggena, who isn't? I
committed myself to spend millions on a
play and then I showed very little
interest in what was happening. For
example, this young, genius playwright I
heard so much about, I had not even met
him at a time when things were beginning
to move along. Sofia had warned me many
times in the past, not about this
Lipshitz fellow specifically, that all
writers are crazy. So what else is new?
Everybody I've ever encountered in any
line of work, I've found to be crazy. The
truth is everybody's crazy - no
exceptions.
                (MORE)

                         MAX (CONT'D)
What confuses some people is that they
see others who seem very normal so they
begin to doubt the 'everybody's crazy
rule' not understanding that the normal
looking ones are the craziest of all. And
all of this is apropos of what? Of my
first meeting, of course, with Scott
Lipshitz who decided to visit me one
evening in my apartment.

The sounds of a door buzzer is heard. MAX, a concerned
look on his face, approaches the door, to his flat.

                         MAX (CONT'D)
Who is it?

                         SCOTT (O.S.)
It's Scott Lipshitz.

                         MAX
Who?

                         SCOTT (O.S.)
Scott Lipshitz, the playwright.

                         MAX
What do you want?

                         SCOTT (O.S.)
I figured I'd come by and introduce
myself.

                         MAX
Ever hear of checking first with the
other party?

                         SCOTT (O.S.)
Well, if it's not convenient I can come
back some other time.

                         MAX
How did you get past the desk man?

                         SCOTT (O.S.)
Well, I just skipped that.

                         MAX
I know that, I asked how.

                         SCOTT (O.S.)
Well, I know how, it's a little hard to
explain.

                    MAX
        I don't find that answer very reassuring.

                    SCOTT (O.S.)
        Don't worry, security in this building is
        good. I can do things others can't.

                    MAX
        Yeah, you're a regular genius, I hear.

He let's SCOTT in. SCOTT enters extending his hand for
handshake.

                    SCOTT
        Hi. I'm Scott.

MAX, without enthusiasm, shakes hi hand. He indicates
opposing chairs, in between a coffee table with a canape
tray. Several canapes are left.

                    SCOTT (CONT'D)
        Sure smells good, what are they?

                    MAX
        Canapes. I made them.

                    SCOTT
        You made them?

                    MAX
        Yes, cooking is my hobby.

                    SCOTT
        That's just wonderful. Wonderful!

                    MAX
        You like to cook, too?

                    SCOTT
            (shakes his head no)
        But, I sure like to eat.

MAX slides the tray to SCOTT who gobbles up a canape with
gusto.

                    MAX
        Finish the rest if you like...

SCOTT grabs and devours the remaining canapes, then pats
his lips with a napkin. A pause.

                    MAX (CONT'D)
        I want to be clear, Scott, I don't want
        you popping in uninvited again.

                    SCOTT
You're right. It's just that I knew
you're a bachelor, and it's early in the
evening, so I figured it would probably
be okay.

                    MAX
So, you do understand the concept of
privacy?

                    SCOTT
Sure.

                    MAX
All right, enough said. (Beat) So, how
did you happen to become a writer?

                    SCOTT
I'm not that crazy about hard work.
Sitting in a comfortable room typing is
better than going out to work. And, I can
take a nap whenever I like.

                    MAX
That's gotta be a breakthrough in
understanding the soul of an artist.

Beat

                    SCOTT
Did you ever go out with June?

                    MAX
What? What's that all about?

                    SCOTT
June. You know who June is?

                    MAX
Yes, I do. And why are you bringing her
up out of a clear blue sky? Did she say
anything to you about me?

                    SCOTT
No. I just had a hunch you'd make a nice
couple.

                    MAX
A hunch?

                    SCOTT
My hunches gotta be taken seriously.

                    MAX
Maybe you oughta take your hunch and
leave.

                    SCOTT
Hey, why are you so excited. I meant
well. And from your reaction you must
like her a lot.

                    MAX
Yes, I do. But, I don't think I'm her
type.

                    SCOTT
Why not?

                    MAX
She's young and beautiful...and I'm not
her type.

                    SCOTT
You're rich.

                    MAX
I don't think that will make a difference
to her.

                    SCOTT
Depends if you know how to play it.

                    MAX
What do you mean?

                    SCOTT
What does June like, what are her main
interests

                    MAX
(thinks) Theatre, the arts, that stuff.

                    SCOTT
Right. You oughta start a foundation for
the arts, something like that, and put
her in charge. You give a woman her dream
and she'll love you to pieces. Trust me.

                    MAX
Why should I trust you? From what I've
heard, you hang around her a lot.

                    SCOTT
It's just platonic.

                    MAX
          Don't tell me she's not interested in
          you.

                    SCOTT
          She is. But it's not good. The play has
          given her the wrong idea about who I
          really am. Say, you don't by an chance
          have more of those canapes?

MAX shakes his head no. Scott rises.

                    SCOTT (CONT'D)
          I think you're ready for me to leave.

SCOTT is at the door.

                    SCOTT (CONT'D)
          How do you like being rich?

                    MAX
          It's very nice.

                    SCOTT
          But, it's kind of a joke, isn't it?

                    MAX
          A joke?

                    SCOTT
          Well, you've heard the expression, 'You
          can't take it with you?"

                    MAX
          I have heard the expression.

                    SCOTT
          Rich people worry about getting cancer
          and dying just like everyone else.

                    MAX
          So?

                    SCOTT
          So, when you're full of yourself and it's
          time to die it must be harder than for us
          ordinary slobs. Don't you think?

                    MAX
          Good night, Mr. Lipshitz.

                    SCOTT
          Good night...what do they call backers of
          Broadway shows? Angels? Good night, my
          angel.

Lights fade here as JUNE enters.

                    JUNE
                (to audience)
          Max telephoned me. He invited me to
          dinner saying he had something important
          he wanted to discuss with me. That was a
          surprise, seeing that I didn't know him
          that well. I just knew him casually
          through Sofia. I just thought of him as a
          pleasant man and I never suspected he was
          interested in my...opinion. Earlier that
          day Sofia told me that later she wanted
          to discuss something important with me.
          Suddenly it seems people had important
          things to say to me.

SOFIA enters.

                    SOFIA
                (to June)
          There's something I need to tell you.
          I've been thinking about how to tell you,
          that is after I decided that I would tell
          you.

                    JUNE
          You're confusing me.

                    SOFIA
          Yeah, that's what comes of over-preparing

                    JUNE
          Since when do you have to prepare to tell
          me something.

                    SOFIA
          Scott and I are lovers.

                    JUNE
          You and Scott...

                    SOFIA
          Yes.

                    JUNE
          Why are you telling me...

                    SOFIA
     I know you like him a lot...

                    JUNE
     It's that obvious?

                    SOFIA
     Of course. You don't try to conceal it.

                    JUNE
     But why does that create an obligation
     for you to...

                    SOFIA
     June, you and I are close friends. I care
     about you.

                    JUNE
     Why are you telling me about this? I
     don't want to know this.

                    SOFIA
     I said I need to tell you, more
     important, I think you need to know.

                    JUNE
     And why is that?

                    SOFIA
     Because we're not in love. I don't even
     think we like each other that much. To
     me, when I think about our relationship,
     it's ridiculous. I'm more apt to laugh
     about it than remotely take it seriously.
     That's what I want you to know.

                    JUNE
     Okay, thank you.

JUNE begins to leave.

                    SOFIA
     I wish you would understand.

                    JUNE
     I wish I could.

                    SOFIA
     June, please...

JUNE stops.

                    SOFIA (CONT'D)
It doesn't mean anything to Scott or to
me. It's not important, I want to get
that across to you.

                    JUNE
All right, so you just do it for the sex.

                    SOFIA
But you see I haven't been sexually
active for years. It wasn't part of my
life. I stopped thinking about it. Yes, I
enjoy it, but it's not that important to
either of us. We laugh when we're doing
it.

                    JUNE
Go to hell.

JUNE exits.

                    SOFIA
                 (to audience)
Well, I tried. I tried to do what? I'm
not so sure myself. It's strange. We get
so smug about knowing ourselves, at least
I did. After all, if you don't know
yourself, then what do you know? I
thought I contained no mysteries from
myself, only to learn I haven't a clue as
to what I'm capable of doing or even why.

SOFIA exits. JUNE enters.

                    JUNE
                 (to audience)
I wanted to quit my job with Sofia then
and there, but even in hot blood common
sense prevailed. If I severed relations
with Sofia, it would mean giving up my
role in the play's production, and in all
probability severing my contact with
Scott and that I would not do under any
circumstances.

JUNE exits. Lights up on a table in a restaurant. Max is
seated alone.

                    MAX
                 (to audience)
June accepted my invitation. We met in a
restaurant since I thought it was
inappropriate to invite her to my place.
                 (MORE)

                    MAX (CONT'D)
She was pleasant throughout the meal but
it was also clear she was a little sad
and preoccupied. My plan was to wait
until we were ready to order desert to
tell her about my idea, but at that point
she excused herself to check on her dog
which she had left in her car in the
restaurant parking lot.

JUNE enters and sits opposite MAX.

                    MAX (CONT'D)
                 (to June)
How's your doggy?

                    JUNE
She's happy.

                    MAX
Well, you've waited patiently to learn
what I want to discuss so I'll get right
to the point.

                    JUNE
I admit I'm curious.

                    MAX
Well, it's no secret that I've amassed a
large fortune. And, I want to start doing
some useful things with my money now.
What I had in mind was a foundation of
some kind that would benefit the arts,
but I'm not sure what I want. And for
starters I thought I would ask you to
come up with some ideas, present them to
me, and then we could go from there.

                    JUNE
Wow, what an exciting idea.

                    MAX
You like it?

                    JUNE
Of course. But, Max, I haven't got the
background to get involved in this.

                    MAX
Uh uh, don't be negative. All I'm asking
right now is that you do some creative
thinking, come up with ideas, concepts,
and run them by me.
                 (MORE)

                    MAX (CONT'D)
When we have a good idea what we want to
do, then the lawyers and accountants and
other professionals come in.

                    JUNE
Gee, Max, I'm speechless.

                    MAX
You don't have to make any commitments
now, just promise me that you'll turn
your mind loose on this project. I don't
care how sketchy your ideas are, I want
to consider them.

                    JUNE
I'm speechless...(beat) Have you asked
Sofia to help with this?

                    MAX
No.

                    JUNE
Why not? She's really sharp.

                    MAX
To be honest, it never occurred to me.

                    JUNE
Why not?

                    MAX
She's a well-established literary agent,
that's what she is. I never gave a
thought to involving her in this. I have
no intention of doing so.

                    JUNE
I'm surprised you didn't ask her.

                    MAX
No. To tell the truth, June, when I
started to consider this idea, it never
occurred to me I would ask anyone but
you. You see, when we're ready to go
forward with this, I want you to head up
the entire thing.

                    JUNE
I'm speechless.

Impulsively, she kisses him on the cheek. He is beaming.
The lights go down on restaurant area. SOFIA enters.

                    SOFIA
               (to audience)
     When I first learned what Max and June
     were getting involved in, I was
     incredulous and I was furious. How could
     he not have told me about his plan and
     how could he not have involved me in it.
     But then, and I'm glad I never let him
     discover how I felt, a little light went
     on. Of course, there had been subtle,
     little signs that Max was sweet on June
     and that he had been too shy even to
     confide in me but now, obviously, he had
     found a way to make a connection. So good
     for him. Besides, wasn't he prepared to
     pump millions into my little project. No
     need to be greedy or unreasonable. So
     life went on, Max and June were getting
     together frequently for an exchange of
     ideas, Scott was still June's regular
     guest for lunch, and mine for dinner, and
     other recreational activities. And now we
     were awaiting the momentary arrival of
     Alistair Cross, believed by many to be
     the preeminent director in the English
     speaking world. He had read Scott's
     script, fallen madly in love with it, was
     available, and was now en route to New
     York just dying to meet our genius
     playwright, Scott Lipshitz, and get to
     work.

SOFIA exits as Alistair Cross enters opposite. He is in
his mid-thirties and speaks with an English accent. He
comes all the way downstage and looks out at the empty
house. He is holding a loose leaf binder which is about
three inches think. All the way upstage, Scott is seated
behind a bridge table. His torso sprawled forward, his
head cradled in his arm, sleeping. The Light is so poor
he is barely visible, certainly Alistair is unaware of
Scott's presence.

                    ALISTAIR
     Whenever I step out on the stage in an
     empty theatre my heart races, pitter
     patter, pitter patter, audibly, rapidly.
     It is some measure of the excitement I
     always feel. Theatre, the theatre, this
     theatre, a theatre, any theatre, no
     matter.
                    (MORE)

                    ALISTAIR (CONT'D)
          Whether it is the embodiment of the idea
          of theatre or the physical plant, no
          matter, for theatre is my life, my
          cathedral, my shrine, my hostel, my
          refuge, my workplace, my home where my
          heart is. What a pity it plays such a
          negligible part in the lives of our
          fellow citizens today. Theatre can give
          us what movies and television cannot
          give. It can challenge us, confront us,
          chasten us, excite us, exhaust us,
          deceive us, enlighten us, amuse us. It is
          the place where we examine our human
          condition in concert with our fellow
          human sojourners, where we willingly
          suspend our will to disbelieve, where we
          are naked together and unashamed, and
          where we emerge, at times, our very souls
          enriched by the experience.

The sound of snoring is heard. Alistair traces the sound
to Scott's table and becomes aware of his presence.

                    ALISTAIR (CONT'D)
          Mr. Lipshitz? So...

Slowly, SCOTT sits up. He looks awful. He emits an
enormous belch that resounds in the empty theatre and
literally causes Alistair to jump backward.

                    SCOTT
          Boy, I needed that. I had three hot dogs
          earlier, kind of wolfed them down,
          doesn't usually bother me 'cause I got a
          cast iron stomach, but every once in a
          while...

He begins to jump up and down in place.

                    ALISTAIR
          What are you doing?

                    SCOTT
          Trying to settle my stomach.

                    ALISTAIR
          That looks a mite unsettling.

                    SCOTT
          It usually works...

SCOTT stops

> SCOTT (CONT'D)
> ...yeah, that's better.

> ALISTAIR
> You're better now?

> SCOTT
> Yeah, sure.

> ALISTAIR
> I'm Alistair Cross.

> SCOTT
> I'm Scott Lipshitz.

They shake hands.

> ALISTAIR
> You're really feeling better now?

> SCOTT
> Yeah, I'm okay. I tell you I've got an
> iron constitution, well almost.

> ALISTAIR
> Oh, good. Well, I can't even begin to
> tell you how much I've been looking
> forward to meeting you. And as for my
> opinion of your play - you've heard I'm
> sure, it's a masterpiece, nothing less.

> SCOTT
> Oh, yeah, thanks.

> ALISTAIR
> I look forward to many stimulating hours
> discussing your play with you. I hope we
> can complete our conversations before we
> need to begin casting.

> SCOTT
> But didn't they tell you...

> ALISTAIR
> Who are 'they' and what were 'they'
> supposed to tell me?

> SCOTT
> Sofia and June. Didn't they tell you I
> never discuss the play?

> ALISTAIR
> No. Of course not. What are you talking
> about?

> SCOTT
> I never discuss the play. I won't discuss
> the play.

> ALISTAIR
> That's ridiculous. See here, I know these
> sessions between writer and director are
> sometimes difficult, tempers flare,
> sensibilities get crushed. Butt nerve
> wracking as they may be, these sessions
> are necessary to pull out the best the
> play has to offer.

> SCOTT
> That's all too complicated, the writer
> writes, the director directs and that's
> all there is to it.

> ALISTAIR
> I've never known a writer like you, don't
> you want to protect, to project your
> vision of your play?

> SCOTT
> Here's the writer's vision. Nothing can
> top that.

SCOTT holds up his script.

> ALISTAIR
> And here are the director's notes. Which
> he needs to review with you.

ALISTAIR holds up his thick notebook.

> SCOTT
> Forget it.

> ALISTAIR
> Forget it? I will not forget it. And what
> of necessary changes when the play is in
> rehearsal? There never was a play that
> didn't need changes during rehearsal.

> SCOTT
> Forget that, too. I will not change a
> single word. Not a single comma, and you
> should know this, you're beginning to
> annoy me.

SCOTT exits. ALISTAIR is plotzing. After fuming and
fulminating for a few minutes, he exits.

MAX enters.

>   MAX
>   (to audience)
>   So this meshuggena director calls me
>   crying, incoherent, he's not happy with
>   our Mr. Lipshitz. Look, I said, I provide
>   money, not a shoulder to cry on. So, bug
>   off.

SOFIA enters.

>   SOFIA
>   (to audience)
>   Alistair called me. He was inconsolable.

JUNE enters.

>   JUNE
>   (to audience)
>   Alistair called me. He was inconsolable.

>   SOFIA
>   (to audience)
>   He demanded a meeting. I persuaded Max to
>   attend, but I didn't succeed with Scott.
>   June, of course, was willing.

ALISTAIR enters. He addresses all of them.

>   ALISTAIR
>   It is unacceptable, it is completely
>   unacceptable. I have never been so
>   humiliated in my life, I my entire life,
>   it is the most egregious behavior I have
>   ever experienced...

>   MAX
>   Egregious?

No one reacts.

>   ALISTAIR
>   I have no choice, I cannot continue, this
>   is my notice to all of you, I am
>   returning to England.

>   MAX
>   Good.

>   SOFIA & JUNE
>   Max!

>   MAX
>   It's obvious he's not happy. No one
>   should have to suffer like that.

JUNE places her hand on MAX'S arm and guides him away.

               JUNE
(to Max) He's just ventilating.

               MAX
Oh, that's what he's doing. Couldn't he
go ventilate somewhere else, like in
England?

               SOFIA
Alistair, you're justified in feeling the
way you do, no doubt about it. But, if
you will get off this emotional roller
coaster, stop and think for a moment,
you'll realize there are distinct
benefits...

               ALISTAIR

Benefits?

               SOFIA
Of course.

               ALISTAIR
What benefits?

               SOFIA
You have a free hand. You don't need to
engage in these knock-down-drag-out
fights with the playwright.

               ALISTAIR
That's true.

               SOFIA
You know how nasty those conflicts can
be.

               ALISTAIR
That's true.

               SOFIA
You see...

               ALISTAIR
But, I need to bounce my ideas off
someone. That's part of the process; It's
how I work.

                    SOFIA
          Okay, you got June and me. June is a
          great dramaturge, and I'm no slouch
          myself. And you can work with us without
          recriminations... I hope.

                    ALISTAIR
          But what about script changes? Legally,
          we can't touch the script without his
          consent. We're stymied.

All look to MAX.

                    MAX
          Not to worry. My lawyer's bigger than the
          other fellow's. Do what you have to do.

                    ALISTAIR
          All right, we'll go forward. Onward!
          Onward!

                    MAX
          Onward Jewish soldiers.

As the lights dim, JUNE comes downstage, SOFIA and MAX go
all the way upstage and ALISTAIR exits.

                    JUNE
                    (to audience)
          Everything was moving right along.
          Alistair was really a take charge fellow
          and he soon discovered the joy that comes
          from an absent playwright. Mainly, we got
          the cast we wanted and, as it turned out,
          Sofia and I worked well with Alistair.
          Even when he was being unreasonable, he
          was reasonably unreasonable. Scott's
          luncheon appearances dropped off,
          although when he did show up he seemed
          more relaxed and congenial than before.
          But he never asked about the play's
          progress or make any reference to it,
          even obliquely. It were as though this
          subject had just simply fallen off his
          radar screen. I was fascinated by his
          behavior but knew better than to broach
          the subject. And I have to confess, I
          never got over the thrill I experienced
          just being in his presence.

JUNE exits. SOFIA comes down stage

                         SOFIA
                    (to audience)
          It was exasperating at times, but mostly
          it went well. Sure, Alistair was a royal
          pain, but what can you expect, he's a
          'director.' June seemed to have gotten
          over her pique with me, at least there
          were no open signs of hostility. Scott
          was not coming over as often for dinner
          and other 'recreational' activities,
          which was okay with me. I was happy when
          he came over and I was just as happy when
          he didn't come. For me, kind of a no-lose
          situation. I was fascinated, however, by
          his complete disinterest in the play.
          Once I said to him, 'Hey, you never ask
          about the progress of the rehearsals,
          don't you have any interest in your play
          at all' to which he replied dismissively,
          'that's okay.' End of conversation. Scott
          Lipshitz, it's fair to say was an enigma.

SOFIA exits.

                         MAX
                    (to audience)
          June and I were meeting pretty often to
          talk about our project. We'd grown
          comfortable with each other, at times
          we'd kick-back, laugh...no question she
          was excited about the foundation for the
          arts idea and she was also excited about
          her part in shaping the Lipshitz play.
          Sometimes, I'd feel a glimmer of hope
          that our 'friendship' could develop, but,
          soon I'd crash to earth realizing she was
          still obsessed with that playwright. How
          did I know? She never talked about him, I
          knew.

MAX exits. JUNE enters.

                         JUNE
                    (to audience)
          Scott was waiting for me outside the
          building one afternoon when I left for
          lunch. For the first time he had departed
          from his usual routine. He had actually
          gone to the deli himself and purchased
          sandwiches to go. He said it was a nice
          day and could we eat the lunch he had
          brought in the park. I agreed.

SCOTT enters and joins JUNE. Together, they walk to a
park bench and sit down. SCOTT removes the sandwiches
from the bag and hands one to her. She inspects it and
indicates her satisfaction. They begin to eat.

                    SCOTT
          (mouth full of food)
          There's something I have to tell you.

                    JUNE
          Oh?

He has taken a large bite from his sandwich and his cheek
is puffed out as he chews. He points his finger at the
side of his face signaling he needs to finish chewing
before he can speak. Finally.

                    SCOTT
          You're a fool. And I don't think I can
          help you.

                    JUNE
          I don't recall asking you for help...or
          your opinion for that matter.

                    SCOTT
          Sometimes I help people who don't know
          they need help.

                    JUNE
          Scott, what's this all about?

                    SCOTT
          It's about your stupid obsession with a
          certain playwright, just because he
          happened to write a play you like. Well,
          I got news for you, there's nothing
          special about writers - no matter how
          talented they are, they're no better or
          worse than anyone else. This writer, you
          don't really know him, he could be a
          serial killer for all you know.

                    JUNE
          You're wrong, I do know this playwright.
          I know him by what he reveals in his
          play. I know he's a beautiful person,
          and, gentle, witty, warm. He cares about
          his fellow human beings, he cares about
          the world he lives in, he is above all a
          caring, loving person.

                    SCOTT
          Bullshit.

                    JUNE
Scott, why do you do this, why do you
posture the way you do? Why do you make
such an effort to deny who you really
are?

                    SCOTT
I'm an impostor, I don't deny that.

                    JUNE
I don't understand.

                    SCOTT
I didn't write the play.

                    JUNE
You didn't...

                    SCOTT
I didn't write the play, I haven't even
read it. What's more, I don't intend to
read the stupid thing.

                    JUNE
I can't believe this.

                    SCOTT
Believe it.

A long pause

                    JUNE
I think I'm entitled to an explanation.

                    SCOTT
Sure you are.

Again, he has taken a large bite from his sandwich and
his mouth is full. He indicates his protruding cheek,
chews rapidly, signalling her to wait a minute.
Finally...

                    SCOTT (CONT'D)
I was a bum, living on the street. I met
this guy, he was dying of AIDS. He told
me he made up his mind no matter what
happened he would never return to the
hospital. He said he had a big apartment
and I could come and stay with him in
exchange for taking care of him when he
couldn't get out of bed.
                    (MORE)

                    SCOTT (CONT'D)
He said I could stay as long as he lived
and because he didn't have any relatives
or any friends left I could keep all his
stuff when he died. His computer, his
clothes and a few thousand bucks he had
left. I went to stay with him. He was a
brave guy. When he could he would get out
of bed and work on his play. He finished
it the day before he died. Just before he
died he told me he didn't get the play
right and he made me promise to destroy
it. But what I did when he was gone, I
substituted a new title page with my
name.

                    JUNE
You violated your promise to a dying man.

                    SCOTT
Sometimes I have a little problem keeping
my word.

                    JUNE
This is incredible.

                    SCOTT
You don't know the half of what goes on
out there.

                    JUNE
You deceived us.

                    SCOTT
Sometimes I have a little problem telling
the truth.

                    JUNE
You deceived me.

                    SCOTT
You helped. Mostly, you deceived
yourself.

                    JUNE
What a fool I've been.

                    SCOTT
If you remember, that's how I started
this conversation.

                    JUNE
You've made your point, now let me make
mine.
                    (MORE)

                    JUNE (CONT'D)
You're a loathesome creature and I hate
you! I hate you! I hate you! I never want
to see you again.

She exits. He is unflappable. After a moment, his eyes
fall on the sandwich she left on the bench. He picks it
up and examines it. It is intact but for one missing
bite. He begins to devour the sandwich.

BLACKOUT

LIGHTS UP on SOFIA.

                    SOFIA
               (to audience)
June told me what happened. I told the
others and we had a meeting.

ALISTAIR, JUNE and MAX enter

                    ALISTAIR
               (very agitated)
It's a disaster, an unmitigated disaster!
Yes, a disaster, that's what it is,
nothing less. A disaster!

                    MAX
               (to the others)
He's being redundant.

                    ALISTAIR
Well, that's it, I'm finished. I will not
be part of this charade. No more, finito,
caput, terminado. I'm out of here.

                    MAX
               (to the others)
He's just ventilating.

                    ALISTAIR
I am planning a lifetime in this
profession and I will not allow my
reputation to be soiled by linking it to
this grand deception. This play is
opening next week and we are representing
to the world that a certain playwright
who we know did not write the play is in
fact the playwright. I will not
participate in this fraud.

                    MAX
              (asserting himself)
     Alright, Alistair, stop making such a
     commotion There is no fraud, no deception
     so just shut up about that.

                    ALISTAIR
     There certainly is, he told June he is
     not he writer.

                    MAX
     And he also represented to all of us over
     a period of months that he was the
     author, and we dealt with him in good
     faith. Why should we automatically assume
     he's telling the truth now and not
     previously? As soon as we find this
     fellow, who seems to have disappeared,
     we'll clear it up. In the meantime, any
     payments due the playwright will be
     placed in a trust fund. Alistair, old
     fellow, stick to directing, do a good job
     and your reputation will be intact. We'll
     worry about the rest.

                    ALISTAIR
              (somewhat mollified)
     Suppose we don't find him?

                    SOFIA
     Don't worry, our playwright has a
     propensity for just popping up,
     especially if there's food nearby. In any
     case, he did join the Dramatists Guild so
     if we don't clear this up we'll just dump
     it in the Guild's lap.

                    ALISTAIR
     But...

                    SOFIA
     But me no buts. And remember this, in the
     hoary tradition of the theatre, hoary - h-
     o-a-r-y- the show must go on!

     JUNE, MAX, ALISTAIR and SOFIA exit. In a moment, SCOTT
     enters and advances downstage center.

                    SCOTT
              (flamboyantly)
     To be or not to be...that is the
     question. Whether...

From off stage the sound of a door slamming is heard.
Scott scoots away and exits. Off stage, JUNE's voice is
heard.

                    JUNE (O.S.)
          I'm sure I left them here. I hope so
          because my extra pair is broken.

JUNE, accompanied by MAX, come up on stage. They go to
the table downstage on which there are some scripts and a
pair of glasses.

                    JUNE (CONT'D)
          Oh, here they are, I'm relieved.

She holds them for MAX to see.

                    MAX
          I'm glad you found them.

She puts on the glasses and looks at MAX

                    JUNE
          The better to see you with, my dear.

                    MAX
          I thought they were reading glasses.

                    JUNE

          They are.

She removes the glasses and slips them in her purse. She
walks downstage and looks out at the auditorium , then
she looks up at MAX, now at her side.

                    JUNE (CONT'D)
          When I was a teenager I flirted with the
          idea of becoming an actress. Boy, for me
          that would have been a mistake. But, you
          know, whenever I step on the stage of an
          empty theatre and look out at the
          auditorium, it's exciting, a strange
          energy envelops me. I can understand why
          so many are drawn to this profession. Do
          you feel it, too?

                    MAX
               (looking at June)
          I feel the magic.

A pause. She glances at him and smiles.

                         MAX (CONT'D)
          June, can I ask you....there's Something
          I'd like to....well, I don't want to
          embarrass you, or myself, uh...you see,
          well, I think you know I like...well,
          what I wanted to ask ...do you think...do
          you think you could...

                         JUNE
          Yes.

They embrace shyly. As they exit, JUNE slips her arm
through his. They appear happy.

ALISTAIR enters.

                         ALISTAIR
                    (to audience)
          The play opened to mixed reviews. No,
          that doesn't adequately describe it.
          Generally, the reviews were respectful
          and quite good. One review , in an
          obscure literary journal, said the play
          was a masterpiece and the directing was
          brilliant. That didn't make me mad. It
          went on to discuss the play, however, in
          such abstruse language, I couldn't
          understand most of it myself. Curiously,
          all he main stream reviewers in
          discussing the play used the term
          'flawed.' As it happens, I don't take
          offense at that term. To me, although it
          may not be the strict dictionary
          definition, the term means perfect but
          for a slight defect. Well, that's about
          as good as things can get in human
          affairs, and I can live with that...I
          think.

MAX has entered.

                         MAX
                    (to audience)
          Lipshitz is still missing. I hired a
          detective to locate him and to find out
          about his past as well. He said the
          assignment was a piece of cake. When he
          reported back to me he was not so cocky.
          In short, he learned nothing about his
          past identity or his present whereabouts.
          Zilch. He was, according to my chagrined
          sleuth, a phantom.
                         (MORE)

                         MAX (CONT'D)
The only concrete thing he learned had to
do with the occupancy of his apartment
for the last six months Neighbors
reported Lipshitz lived alone. He left he
apartment only to walk to the corner
market and he would be seen returning
with an overflowing bag of groceries in
each arm. No one came to his apartment
except pizza deliver persons and the
like. He had a front apartment and most
of the time he could be seen sitting at a
desk at the front window typing. That's
it , and certainly it does not track with
the story he told June. Scott Lipshitz
remains a mystery. Interesting fellow,
our Mr. Lipshitz.

JUNE has entered.

                         JUNE
                    (to audience)
He was right, of course, when he called
me a fool. It hurt terribly at the time
but it makes me smile now. And I know I
have reason to be grateful to Scott,
surely I got value received for those
lunches I bought him. From Scott I
learned, though the lessons were never
explicit, in fact, they were delivered by
some sort of osmosis - the lessons, don't
be a snob and an elitist, don't fall into
a rut and stay there. Don't let your
conceits rule your life. Develop an
appetite for many things. Well, I'm
working on that, and I've never been
happier in my life.

SOFIA has entered.

                         SOFIA
                    (to audience)
The play is drawing pretty good houses.
There's still a good possibility the
audiences will begin to build here
through word of mouth. It's a lovely play
and we're all proud to be part of it
except who knows what he-with-the-
unfortunate-surname thinks about all
this. Well, I enjoyed him while he was on
the scene. Through him I recovered my
lost sexuality although how it got lost
in the first place I can't be sure.
                         (MORE)

                    SOFIA (CONT'D)
Not that I plan on becoming a wanton
woman, well maybe I will....let's face it
I'm a lusty creature.

                    ALISTAIR
              (to audience)
One of the reviewers said regarding the
theme of the play, 'it punctures the
bubble of the pretentiousness.' He said
the main theme dealt with avoiding narrow
and sterile lives, avoiding the twin
evils of stasis and inertia and allowing
ourselves to break out and live self-
fulfilling lives. That was not what I had
focused on mostly in my interpretation of
the play but surely it is valid. That's
the genius of this play, its multiple
themes and levels, the wonderful mosaic
it weaves into a tapestry of id...whoa!
Mosaic and tapestry? Isn't that a clumsy
mixed metaphor if it even rises to that
level? But, what the hell? I'm not a
playwright, thank God, I'm a *director*.

                    MAX
              (to audience)
My life has not been lacking in
achievements and rewards. I've been on
the cover of Time and Newsweek. The Wall
Street Journal did a series of articles
about me, very favorable. I've slept in
the Lincoln bedroom, well, I think I'll
give up my bragging rights to that one.
But, nothing in my life comes close to
the happiness of being in love. Love,
there's nothing like it, nothing comes
close. It's the only thing, in my
opinion, that makes our short ride on
this small planet worthwhile. Love.

                    JUNE
              (to audience)
I love Max.

                    SOFIA
              (to audience)
I love... life.

MAX and JUNE exit, stage right. SOFIA and ALISTAIR exit,
stage left. SCOTT enters from the center. He is wearing a
tuxedo resplendent with glittering rhinestones. He is
holding a large manila envelop, the exact size and
thickness of the envelope we saw early in the play. He
comes all the way downstage and stops.

There is a strange grin on his face. He is about to speak when the shouts of a food vendor are heard off stage and just outside the building.

> VENDOR (O.S.)
> Hey, red hots, red hots, get your red
> hots here!

SCOTT turns in the direction of the shouts. Excited, he flails his arms overhead.

> SCOTT
> Hey! Give me three, with everything and
> plenty of extra mustard!

He exits running in the direction of the vendor's voice.

END OF PLAY

www.ingramcontent.com/pod-product-compliance
Lightning Source LLC
Chambersburg PA
CBHW081326090426
42737CB00017B/3040